AN INQUIRY
INTO THE FORGERY
OF THE
ETRUSCAN
TERRACOTTA WARRIORS

IN THE METROPOLITAN
MUSEUM OF ART

AN INQUIRY INTO THE FORGERY

OF THE

ETRUSCAN

TERRACOTTA WARRIORS

IN THE METROPOLITAN

MUSEUM OF ART

BY DIETRICH VON BOTHMER
AND JOSEPH V. NOBLE

Papers · *No. 11*

THE METROPOLITAN MUSEUM OF ART
NEW YORK · 1961

Of this monograph
issued as
PAPERS NO. 11
2000 copies were printed
December 1961 by the
Plantin Press

FOREWORD

The three terracotta sculptures of Etruscan warriors, acquired in 1915, 1916, and 1921, were first placed on exhibition in 1933 and briefly announced in the Museum's *Bulletin*. Four years later they were fully published by Gisela M. A. Richter, then Curator of Greek and Roman Art, in the Metropolitan Museum "Papers." Spectacular finds of such importance for the history of an early civilization aroused suspicions forthwith, and questions about the statues' authenticity began to be raised. Massimo Pallottino, for instance, condemned the sculptures as forgeries in *Roma* of December 1937 and repeated his charges in 1954. For years such denunciations of the warriors continued, but reports of their modern origin were based on suspicion or hearsay. Despite continued inquiries both in this country and in Europe by members of the Museum's staff and administration, no concrete proof of the various allegations was forthcoming. Several distinguished scholars continued to believe that the warriors had been made in ancient Etruria.

It was not until recently that Joseph V. Noble, Operating Administrator of the Museum, was able to apply the data he had obtained on the technique of Attic vase painting to the technical problems of the manufacture of the warriors and related pieces. His studies provided the first technical evidence of their having been made in modern times. This evidence was completely corroborated on January 5, 1961, when Alfredo Adolfo Fioravanti of Rome signed a sworn statement to the effect that he had participated in the construction of certain terracotta statues in the archaic Etruscan style that were in The Metropolitan Museum of Art. Dietrich von Bothmer, Curator of Greek and Roman Art since 1959, had been studying the statues and was sent to see Mr. Fioravanti without delay. On February 14, the Museum issued the following statement for publication:

> The Metropolitan Museum of Art announced yesterday that, as a result of recently completed studies, its three "Etruscan" terracotta statues must be considered of doubtful authenticity. For some years there have been conflicting claims about these statues based mainly on stylistic grounds. Recently the staff of the Museum began a series of modern scientific and technical analyses. These developed convincing proof that these famous statues were not made in ancient times.
>
> The three terracottas, a large warrior, a smaller warrior, and a large helmeted head, were acquired between 1915 and 1921. They were placed on exhibition in 1933 and published for the first time in the Museum *Bulletin* for February of that year. They are presently on exhibition on the second floor of the South Wing of the Museum.
>
> The Museum stated that a full report of the results of all its investigations will be published in the near future.

We are now ready to issue the facts leading to the conclusion given in the press release.

That a doubt existed about the authenticity of these handsome concoctions is now of little interest. The facts at hand, as published in this paper, should bring to a close what, alas, is not an isolated chapter in the history of collecting.

JAMES J. RORIMER, *Director*

ACKNOWLEDGMENTS

THE INVESTIGATION and the publication have been made possible through the co-operation of our colleagues in New York and abroad. Brian F. Cook, Assistant Curator of Greek and Roman Art, and Andrew Oliver, Jr., Curatorial Assistant, participated in the last phase of the investigation and helped draft the publication. They, and Marjorie J. Milne, former Research Associate in the Department of Greek and Roman Art, also read the manuscript. Murray Pease, Conservator of The Metropolitan Museum of Art, gave us the benefit of his analytical experience. Sir John Beazley kindly supplied photographs of the warriors taken before they came to New York; Professor Bernard Ashmole made the Warren and Marshall papers at Oxford available. D. E. L. Haynes and R. A. Higgins of the British Museum, Vagn H. Poulsen and Mogens Gjødesen of the Ny Carlsberg Glyptotek, and Professor Jean Charbonneaux and Mme Simone Mollard-Besques of the Louvre supplied specimens of comparative material for spectrographic analyses, greatly facilitated the technical study of objects in their care, and supplied photographs which are here published with their kind permission. Violette Verhoogen of the Musée Cinquantenaire in Brussels, Dr. L. W. Böhm of the Reiss Museum in Mannheim, Hermine Speier of the Vatican, Professor Carlo Pietrangeli of the Capitoline Museum, and Dr. Giorgio Fallani supplied valuable information and photographs. Professor Massimo Pallottino, Professor Michelangelo Cagiano de Azevedo, Dr. Mario Moretti, and Dr. Giuseppe Foti gave much time to several discussions in Rome, allowed a close examination of the terracotta sculptures in the Villa Giulia, and provided us with specimens of the Veii statues for analysis. Professor Arvid Andrén supplied photographs and notes for the discussion of architectural terracottas; Professor H. R. W. Smith helped with the question of Caeretan terracottas. Other specific acknowledgments are made in the text.

DIETRICH VON BOTHMER
JOSEPH V. NOBLE

THE HISTORY OF THE TERRACOTTA WARRIORS

by Dietrich von Bothmer

THE THREE terracotta warriors were bought by John Marshall, a purchasing agent for The Metropolitan Museum of Art from 1906 until his death in 1928. Mr. Marshall, an English archaeologist who lived in Rome, was a salaried member of the staff of the Museum and had complete authority to initiate and to conclude purchases abroad for the Museum out of his annual appropriation. Before acting in this capacity for the Metropolitan Museum, he had for many years worked with Edward P. Warren, an American residing in England, whose purchases for the Museum of Fine Arts in Boston built up the classical collection in that museum. The activities of Mr. Warren and Mr. Marshall were of great advantage to the museums for which they bought. American museums in the early periods of their growth were handicapped by the distances in time and space which separated them from the active centers of the art market. These difficulties were overcome by having a purchasing agent reside in Europe. Mr. Marshall did not merely buy classical antiquities, he also ascertained provenances, dates, and attributions, which were discussed in his conscientious and scholarly reports to Edward Robinson (Director of the Museum from 1910 until his death in 1931 and Curator of Classical Art until 1925) and to Gisela M. A. Richter (Assistant Curator of Classical Art 1910-22, Associate Curator 1922-25, and Curator 1925-48). Mr. Marshall also kept notebooks and diaries, which were willed to Mr. Warren; following Mr. Warren's death, they came to the Ashmolean Museum at Oxford. The following account is based on these sources.

The three terracotta warriors are discussed here in the order of their purchase. The "old warrior,"[1] so called because of his white beard, was acquired in 1915; the "colossal head,"[2] in 1916; and the "big

warrior,"[3] in 1921. In the correspondence they are often referred to as "T.C." (terracotta[s]) and are sometimes called "dolls" or "dollies."

The old warrior (Plates I-III) is first mentioned in a letter from Mr. Marshall to Miss Richter of November 14, 1915: "One thing I have arranged for, if a permesso for it can be obtained. It will make you groan to hear of it: the biggest T.C. you or any reasonable being ever saw. Milani's *Atlante* Tav. XXX will give you an idea of it, but you must multiply the height by 7 (seven!), subtract the shield, add a beard and omit the right arm." The letter arrived December 3, 1915, and Miss Richter replied, "We are looking forward to see the large t.c. of which you speak." The warrior's arrival in about twenty fragments was acknowledged by Mr. Robinson in a cable to Rome on February 4, 1916. A week later Miss Richter wrote Mr. Marshall: "The Etruscan terracotta statue has arrived safely and is at present being put together. I think it is quite exciting and will be one of the most dramatic things in the museum. How beautifully the painted patterns are preserved. Do you know anything of its provenance?" To this Mr. Marshall (through Mr. Warren) cabled from Oxford on March 23, 1916: "Please delay publication large terracotta"; and in a letter from Rome of the same date he tells Miss Richter: "We appreciate how much you would like news of T.C. but I am unable to tell you anything. I am sorry, for you must be impatient. We know of nothing to tell you."

His next purchase, the colossal head (Plates VI-IX) is not described in detail in the letters. It arrived

---

1. Acc. no. 15.164. Height (without plinth) 6 feet 7¾ inches.

2. Acc. no. 16.117. Height 4 feet 7 inches.

3. Acc. no. 21.195. Height (without plinth) 8 feet ¼ inch.

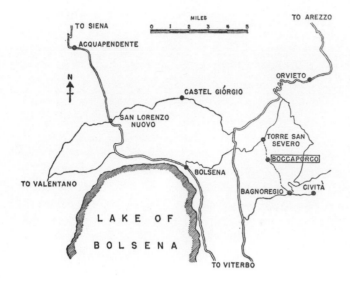

in New York in 178 fragments in four cases on July 25, 1916. Repair work on it was begun in August and completed in October 1916. In January of 1917, Mr. Robinson cabled, "When may terracottas be exhibited and published?" Mr. Marshall and Mr. Warren advised, "Publication must be delayed, exhibition undesirable," to which Mr. Robinson replied, "All right agree entirely." In February 1917, Charles F. Binns, Director of the New York State School of Clay-working and Ceramics at Alfred University (Alfred, New York), the leading ceramic expert in this country, studied a fragment of the colossal head at the request of the Museum.

During the war, communication between Italy and America was difficult, but when Mr. Marshall obtained permission in 1917 to go to England to attend the sale of the Hope collection at Christie's, he took advantage of this opportunity to write at length about the old warrior and the colossal head. In a twenty-two-page letter of August 3, 1917, Mr. Marshall reports to Mr. Robinson as follows: "That head was found at *Boccaporco* which lies on your left as you go on the main road from Orvieto to Bolsena [see map above]. Boccaporco is marked on the 17th century maps, but is only just legible on the big survey maps at present obtainable: it is about 2½ miles from Bagnorea[4] in the direction of Torre San Severo. The men have found large tiles coming from a big temple: they have found the two terra-cottas of Mars [i.e., the old warrior and the colossal head] which you have: a couple of fragments of

4. [Also known as Bagnoregio.]
5. [Published by Edoardo Galli in *Monumenti antichi* XXIV (1916) cols. 5-116, pls. 1-4.]

vases of excellent date, circ. 500, Attic: and great blocks of a base on which your great T.C. 'undoubtedly' stood. This base (which I haven't yet seen) is in *solid* terracotta: rectangular and about a metre high.

"The whole place which was being excavated had to be covered up and sown over with wheat. Nothing can be done till the harvest there is over: but I expect news of some sort when I get back.

"Meanwhile I have been *in the neighbourhood* a great deal, but have never ventured to Boccaporco itself. I am told that the inhabitants of that hamlet have a tradition of a giant who lived on their hill: I think that the man who told me was not lying. What is sure is that the site is quite unknown to the books—I have searched for months in the records. Only, about 7 years ago, near Torre San Severo a sarcophagus[5] of the 4th century was found wonderfully fresh in condition. There was a dispute between Florence and Orvieto as to which of them should have it: pending the decision the sarcophagus was packed up in cotton wool and left in the rain, and finally, when it fell to Orvieto, all the painting on it, or nearly all, had peeled off. Yet, even as it is, it is thought to be one of the most important Etruscan monuments known.

"This sarcophagus was found about 2 kilometres from Boccaporco, 2 kilometres *walk*, but less than 1 as the crow flies. There are traces of old Etruscan roads in the neighbourhood and there are many tombs. But *there is no trace of any town* near, save Bagnorea: and the country between that town and Torre San Severo is so difficult that it is hard to think that our temple of Mars could belong to Bagnorea. I can make no rational suggestions: but I have thought that the two roads, one from Vulci, one from Corneto, coming towards Orvieto on different sides of the lake of Bolsena, may have joined somewhere near Boccaporco.

"At any rate your head is pure Ionic work of about the period to which tradition assigns the Jupiter Capitolinus of the Tarquins. I can find nothing approaching it in importance. There is nothing known of the Jupiter Capitolinus, though it is generally 'supposed' to have been gigantic. The discovery of your head simply demolishes whole volumes of Paio's History of Rome.

"(There are by the way two small fragments of the beard which I am trying to get from one of the excavators.)

"This business has occupied most of my time. The excavators imagine that they are going to find a whole figure 25 feet high of terracotta, and they will not listen to me when I suggest that the body was of wood. Neither have they found the favissae of the temple."

After this long letter nothing more comes up in the correspondence until 1918, when Professor C. Densmore Curtis of the American Academy in Rome returned to America on a brief visit. In a letter to Mr. Robinson of July 13, 1918, Professor Curtis reports that Mr. Marshall "wishes nothing said still about the large t.c. head, but would like me to bring back some photographs of it, if it can be arranged." Professor Curtis returned to Rome late in 1918; on February 28, 1919, he again wrote Mr. Robinson: "We have been more than interested lately over developments more or less connected with those photographs you gave me last summer, though this time of much more importance. The same material is in question, but in high relief, a slab 6 ft. 6 by 20 with about 20 figures in combat or fallen. Some of these are said to have round & some oval shields. There also seems to be a huge reported head of which the helmet crest alone is nearly a meter high."

In another letter to Mr. Robinson, of April 27, 1919, Professor Curtis explains: "We had nothing more to write, not even having seen the objects or a photograph. We hope very soon to know more and will let you know at once."

Two months later Professor Curtis sailed for America, and on his arrival in Boston he at once wrote Mr. Robinson (July 19, 1919): "He [i.e., Marshall] is still hoping to get a huge t.c. figure from the same place, and if he succeeds will come over here at once, if possible on the same boat. It will not be for some months however. There are ever so many details to tell you, but hope I can do so in person. Are you coming to the Archaeological Club meeting? If not let me know and I will write more fully."

Mr. Robinson did not attend the meeting of the club, and on August 1, 1919, Professor Curtis expanded his account as promised: "Marshall himself was leaving for Bagni di Lucca, but had left word that his agents were to telegraph for him in case anything of importance required his presence. They have a huge terracotta statue all excavated, but it is so carefully guarded we could not see it. (It is from the same site as the large t.c. head, of course.) All we could find out about the statue is that it is of a different type than the one in New York, of very heavy build, and that the helmet has a huge well-preserved crest which is modelled but not painted, and reaches far down the back. The site is being worked by three brothers of whom the capable one[6] died in an accident last winter. The one with whom we deal is apparently half crazy[7] [Curtis's literal translation of the milder Italian term *mezzo matto*], so you can imagine that negotiations are difficult and take a long time. M. will get the statue if possible, and if he does will come over here at once, on the same boat if he can."

Next came a cablegram from Mr. Warren to Mr. Robinson, dated August 13, 1919: "John Marshall requested us to telegraph you as follows: Have seen the new find Mars fighting 260 or 270 centimetres high wonderful preservation same artist as big head most important thing ever offered us cannot get photographs price asked quite fantastic."

Later that year Mr. and Mrs. Marshall came to America and stayed until Christmas. There is no further correspondence in 1919, and presumably Mr. Marshall was able to talk about the warrior with Mr. Robinson.

Throughout 1920 Mr. Marshall was kept waiting. In July he wrote Miss Richter from Bagni di Lucca, "I am nailed down to this spot waiting for a big matter." In November 1920, Mr. Robinson sailed for Egypt, but stopped in Rome and saw Mr. Marshall.

During Mr. Robinson's absence the big warrior (Plates x-xv) arrived in fragments in New York. The Purchasing Committee of the Museum met on February 26, 1921 and authorized the purchase of the statue, since the price was more than Mr. Marshall had left in his purchase funds.

Mr. Robinson, on his return to New York, again engaged the services of Mr. Binns, who examined the statue in June and submitted a preliminary report on its construction in July 1921. Mr. Robinson then drafted an article on the construction of the big warrior during the summer of that year.

In the meantime Mr. Marshall had gone to Chianciano for his health. While there he hoped to explore the countryside and to take a trip from Chianciano to Chiusi, thence to Acquapendente, and from there to Bolsena, which would have brought him to the neighborhood of Boccaporco. He had been studying afresh all large-scale Etruscan terracottas, and there is a biggish notebook

---

6. [This was Riccardo Riccardi.]

7. [Either Teodoro Riccardi or his brother Virgilio Angelino.]

among his papers in the Ashmolean Museum which pertains to his work on the big warrior. He noted each ornament, looked for parallels, and collected most of the references to large-scale work in terracotta. He examined the Castellani sarcophagus in the British Museum and the Campana sarcophagus in the Louvre (see Plate XXIV) and expressed his doubts about the authenticity of the former (now known to be a forgery).

By the winter of 1921/22, Mr. Marshall still had not been to the spot where the warriors were said to have been found. His "friends" (the excavators) were sick, he reported, but he expected to be called to the spot "every day." His friends appear next in a letter to Mr. Robinson of October 26, 1924; they had sold behind his back a large collection of vases, bronzes, and terracottas to the Ny Carlsberg Glyptotek,[8] and Mr. Marshall concludes the account by saying, "In that way I have lost touch with the rogues."

There is very little about the warriors in later letters. In August 1926, Mr. Marshall reports that he has "cut all relations with my Orvietans for good."

On February 15, 1928, Mr. Marshall died suddenly in Rome.

Annie Rivier, Mr. Marshall's secretary since the end of the war, continued to work for the Museum, and on June 27, 1928, she reported to Miss Richter, then Curator of the Classical Department, on various transactions, finished and unfinished. Here is what she has to say on the warriors: "Have heard nothing about them for a long time. The sellers, the Riccardi brothers, are watched by the government because they are known to know Etruria thoroughly and to have made excavations with and often without a permit. They have had to quit Orvieto: one is now in Florence; another in Siena. Of the 3rd I know nothing. Their friend the detective has been transferred to Genoa some 2 or 3 years ago. Of the peasants I know nothing. Prof. Paribeni[9] knows that Mr. Marshall had dealings with the Riccardis: about 2 years ago he warned Mr. Marshall against buying from them."

After the death of Mr. Marshall, Miss Richter continued the work on the warriors in preparation of a publication. In April 1929, she had several discussions with Mr. Binns and Maude Robinson (the noted New York potter, at that time Director of the Pottery Department of Greenwich House) and revised the original report on the structure and the technique of the big warrior.

For the next two years Mr. Robinson was much occupied with the installation of the South Wing of the Museum in which part of the classical collection was to be displayed. He was in poor health, and he died on April 18, 1931, after a long illness. When the South Wing of the Museum was opened, plans were made for an Etruscan gallery south of the Roman Court, and it was decided to put off the exhibition and publication of the warriors until the Etruscan gallery was ready. In September 1932, Miss Richter wrote once again to Miss Rivier and asked her to look into the matter of the Attic vase fragments alleged to have been found with them and to collect other information concerning them. Miss Rivier made inquiries of Amedeo Riccardi, but he "could not remember anything definite."

The new Etruscan gallery was opened in February 1933, and the warriors were exhibited for the first time. A brief account of the warriors by Miss Richter appeared in the Museum's February *Bulletin*.[10] This was only a provisional publication, for it was felt that there were many questions not yet fully answered, and it was hoped that Amedeo Riccardi might supply more information. Thus Miss Rivier continued her researches, and on November 12, 1933, she reported that Amedeo Riccardi "talked of the want of proportion between the legs and the top of the figure of your large T.C. warrior; he suggested that it was made on purpose and that the statue must originally have stood on a very high base [see Plate X, right]." To this Miss Richter replied on November 29, 1933: "Many people have made that remark about the legs of the warrior, but shouldn't it be just the other way round? Mr. Casson[11] aptly quoted today that the statue of Nelson in Trafalgar Square has in reality very long legs to make them appear normal at such a height."

After the publication of the warriors in the *Bulletin*, they began to be mentioned in the archaeological literature for this or that detail.[12] Stanley Cas-

---

8. Published by Frederik Poulsen "Aus einer alten Etruskerstadt" in *Det kgl. danske Videnskabernes Selskab, Historisk-filologiske Meddelelser* XII, 3 (1927).

9. [This was Professor Roberto Paribeni.]

10. *The Metropolitan Museum of Art Bulletin* XXVIII (1933) pp. 29 ff.

11. [The late Stanley Casson of Oxford, at that time a visiting professor at Bowdoin College in Brunswick, Maine.]

12. E. g., D. M. Robinson in *American Journal of Archaeology* XXXVIII (1934) p. 501, note 1; E. Kukahn *Der griechische Helm* (1936) p. 108, note 283; F. Poulsen in *Die Antike* XIII (1937) p. 127.

son was eager to publish them in *Antiquity* but was persuaded to await the fuller publication by Miss Richter in the Metropolitan Museum "Papers."

While work on this monograph was in progress, Miss Richter received the first indication of a doubt concerning the authenticity of the warriors. On April 7, 1936, Professor Piero Tozzi, an art dealer with galleries in Florence and New York, wrote Miss Richter from his New York address: "If sometime you happen to be in this neighborhood, I would appreciate very much if you would come and see me. I would gladly come and see you, but being alone, I cannot leave my office during office hours. I have something to tell you which I am sure will interest you to know." At the foot of the page he wrote, "Fioravanti—Riccardi Bros. Teodoro."

As Mr. Tozzi recalls the incident, he had just returned to New York from a trip to Italy, and in Rome he had heard that the Etruscan warriors were forgeries made by Fioravanti and the Riccardis. His knowledge was admittedly not firsthand, but rather based on various anecdotes related to him by friends in the Roman market, especially Aldo Jandolo. Miss Richter was, of course, familiar with the name Riccardi, since the family had been alluded to by Mr. Marshall and named specifically by Miss Rivier. Fioravanti, on the other hand, had never been mentioned before, and Miss Richter immediately wrote Miss Rivier as follows: "There is an absurd story going around that our t.c. dollies are modern and the work of Fioravanti. Aldo [Jandolo] has told Tozzi about it, who told it to me. It is easy to see why such a story should be told, as it makes it more comfortable for many people. And I don't propose to pay any attention to it except to ask you to find out who this Fioravanti is and what kind of things he makes, so that if I am confronted with such a theory I may know about this man."

Here is Miss Rivier's reply (dated May 9, 1936): "With regard to the man you write of on April 24: he began work as a tailor, went on as a car driver; for some time had a small business in old furniture; then went back to his cars; he has been for many years, and still is, a taxi driver in Rome. It does not sound much like an artist. Perhaps I can hear more, but until now this is all. But, as 'il n'y a pas de fumée sans feu' I heard too that he used to make A.'s [Alfredo Barsanti's] clothes and used to drive their car for the family. And many tales have been spread years ago."

A year later, in July 1937, the monograph by Miss Richter, *Etruscan Terracotta Warriors in The Metropolitan Museum of Art*, appeared as the sixth number of the Museum "Papers." It included a report on the structure and technique of the big warrior by Mr. Binns (who had died late in 1934) with revisions by Miss Robinson. This monograph, fully illustrated, received much attention. The findings were accepted and the author was congratulated in numerous reviews.[13] In Italy the publication was first noted in an editorial in *L'Urbe* by Antonio Muñoz in the issue of November 1937, and this mention provoked a discussion in Rome about the authenticity of the warriors. In the December number of the same periodical, Muñoz stated that he had asked Professor Giulio Emanuele Rizzo for his opinion concerning the big warrior, and Rizzo had authorized him to publish that he declared it to be of indisputable authenticity.[14]

The public acclaim of the terracotta warriors, which had now spread to Italy, prompted Massimo Pallottino to register a dissenting opinion. In *Roma* of December 1937,[15] he dismissed all three sculptures in a masterly manner as forgeries. The very bronze statuette from Dodona (Plate XVII) with which Miss Richter had compared the big warrior was considered by Pallottino to be its prototype, its inspiration, and the colossal head was likewise reduced in scale by being compared with the East Greek aryballoi (see Plate VII B, C) in the shape of helmeted heads. For prototypes of the old warrior, Pallottino pointed to the wiry Italo-Etruscan bronze statuettes. His attack on the terracotta warriors did not reach New York. In Italy it angered Professor Rizzo, who summoned Pallottino to his apartment for a dressing down (as recounted in *Il Tempo* of February 24, 1961).

Pallottino's note limited itself to questions of style; a technical approach to the problem of the

---

13. S. Casson in *Journal of Hellenic Studies* LVIII (1938) p. 104; M[arcel] R[enard] in *Latomus* II (1938) p. 221; R. Carpenter in *American Journal of Archaeology* XLIII (1939) pp. 169-70; G. Lippold in *Berliner philologische Wochenschrift* LIX (1939) cols. 1168 ff.; and F. Matz in *Gnomon* XV (1939) pp. 451-52.

14. *Poichè, a quanto ci è stato riferito, alcuni avrebbero espresso l'opinione che si tratti di una volgare falsificazione, abbiamo voluto interrogare in proposito un giudice quanto mai competente o, per meglio dire, il più competente tra i giudici in questa materia, e cioè il prof. Giulio Emanuele Rizzo, il quale ci ha autorizzato a pubblicare che egli dichiara la statua in questione di autenticità indiscutibile.* (Antonio Muñoz in *L'Urbe* II, No. 12 [1937] p. 48.)

15. Pp. 473-74. He repeated his opinion about the warriors' authenticity in *Archeologica classica* VI (1954) p. 170.

warriors' authenticity was employed by Michelangelo Cagiano de Azevedo. Cagiano advanced the theory that the craquelure of the glaze (see Plates XIV, XIX) was in fact the result of a siccative added to a varnish.[16] This hypothesis, proposed before Cagiano had seen the statues himself, was not valid, as the surfaces of all three warriors are entirely free from varnish and have instead fired ceramic colors. A different technical point was mentioned by Pico Cellini, who contended[17] that the statues' clay body contained ground-up glass from Peroni beer bottles. Cellini had seen the warriors and probably examined the surface of the fractures; but the glittering elements of the clay body had been correctly identified by Mr. Binns as quartz. Cellini also asserted that the warriors had been fired in pieces, and tells of a visit to Siena where he made the acquaintance of a former chief of police whom he called Mr. Marshall's intermediary in the acquisition of the warriors. Mr. Cellini's attack was anecdotal in manner and tantalizingly condensed. His conclusions were based on partly wrong evidence, since there were no ground-up beer bottles in the clay of the warriors.

A third technical attack was made verbally in the winter of 1958/59 by the restorer Mario Modestini, who claimed that the black glaze of the warriors was nothing but casein paint. Murray Pease, Conservator of the Metropolitan Museum, made tests that very promptly discounted this theory.

From time to time other scholars and visitors to the Museum made their own observations which did not get into print and were not always communicated to the staff of the Museum. Harold W. Parsons first expressed his doubts in the early forties; Iris C. Love submitted a B.A. thesis at Smith College in 1955 in which she contended that the old warrior was genuine, while the colossal head and the big warrior were modern.[18] In the spring of 1953, Ernest Brummer expressed to me doubts about the big warrior, based on its instability of construction; and during a very brief visit to the Museum in the fall of 1959, Professor Cagiano, refusing to look closely at the warriors, said to me,

"How can I, when I know the man who made them?"

During all these years, however, the warriors continued to be accepted as genuine, not only by American archaeologists, who repeatedly singled them out for republication, but also abroad, notably in Denmark and Germany. Lest the discussion of their authenticity be continued endlessly and fruitlessly on the basis of style or rumor alone, a new approach was clearly in order. The technical investigations that provided an answer to this question are fully discussed in Joseph V. Noble's section of this paper. Foremost among the proofs of the forgeries were the composition of the black glaze of the warriors and the method of their construction. In Germany during the Second World War, Dr. Theodor Schumann had successfully reproduced the ancient classical black glaze and had shown that the color was achieved by a three-stage firing process, rather than by the addition of a coloring agent. At the annual meeting of the Archaeological Institute of America on December 29, 1959, Mr. Noble, Operating Administrator of the Museum, pointed out that the black glaze of forgeries made before Schumann's discovery of the ancient technique would have been colored by an added mineral. Mr. Noble had already begun a series of spectrographic analyses of the warriors (see Appendix B), that showed the presence of manganese, a coloring agent never used in classical ceramics, in the glaze of all three and in the clay body of two of the warriors. Corroborative evidence of the modern origin of the statues was provided by our examinations of authentic Greek, Cypriot, and Etruscan large-scale terracottas: we found that in these the ventilation of the clay mass had always been carefully provided for. But although the warriors had each obviously been made in one piece, it would have been technically impossible to fire them whole: there had been no adequate provision for the circulation of air necessary during the drying and firing of the clay, which, in ancient terracottas, had been assured by a proper disposition of ventholes (see Plate XXIV).

Thus, all questions of style aside, the glaze and technique of firing sufficed to condemn the warriors on scientific grounds. But the story could not be considered complete until other leads had been followed up. Even before the technical analyses were being carried out, the vendors and the history of the purchases were being carefully investigated.

Although the Riccardis did not appear officially

16. In *Bollettino dell' Istituto Centrale del Restauro* I (1950) p. 44.

17. In *Paragone* LXV (May 1955) pp. 46-47.

18. Her stylistic arguments have since been published in an altered form in *Marsyas* IX (1961) pp. 14-35. Following the announcement by the Museum concerning the authenticity of the warriors, she has changed her view of the antiquity of the old warrior.

as the vendors in the Museum records, their connection with the purchases was clear from the correspondence, and any investigation of the provenance and circumstances of the finding had to take into account the part the Riccardis played. Of the Riccardis mentioned or alluded to in the letters of Mr. Marshall, Professor Curtis, and Miss Rivier, only one, Amedeo Ariodante Riccardi, was still alive. In the fall of 1955, Christine Alexander, who had succeeded Miss Richter as Curator of Greek and Roman Art in 1948, had visited Amedeo Riccardi in Florence and pressed him for additional information concerning the statues or their discovery. Riccardi made a sketch map of the area of Boccaporco where the warriors were said to have been found and identified the proprietors of the land. He stressed the difficulties of going to Boccaporco—the roads were bad and the locality could not be reached by car. He promised, however, to take up the matter and for the next five years was in touch with Miss Richter in Rome. He visited Miss Richter on March 5, 1958, and here is her report to James J. Rorimer, Director of the Museum since 1955: "R. told me again what he had said before, namely that neither his brother nor his father (there are two versions) had ever been engaged in making t.c. statues; that our warriors were found in the neighborhood of Orvieto, and that the finder (scavatore) was a certain Campanella, who died in 1928 and who had also found the polychrome sarcophagus now in the Orvieto Museum (likewise suspected by some).[19] I understand he told you all this himself in Florence, as well as to Miss Alexander when she saw him 2½ years ago, and I am glad that both of you have heard the story direct from R. and can form an opinion of it. The story has never varied in any particular and seems consistent with what Marshall told us.

"I told Riccardi, however, that we now want 'factual' evidence to meet whatever evidence will be produced by the other side, and asked him to find out whether any member of the Campanella family was still alive (the son is also dead it seems) and could produce *facts*; also, as you know, I plan to go (with him) to the spot where he was told the figures were found (a fountain, however, is said to have been built there).

"One obvious inconsistency in the stories told about the warriors is that on the one hand it is claimed they were seen here in Rome all complete 38 years ago (this has been changed somewhat by now, it seems), and on the other hand that they

were fired in pieces (Cellini). R. promises to do his best to produce the evidence needed and will let me know. I shall keep you informed." In a postscript Miss Richter adds: "What about Cellini's claim (*Due Appunti . . .* p. 11) that the t.c. of the warriors contains pulverized parts of Peroni beer bottles? That could easily be countered."

In September 1958, Herbert Hoffmann joined the Museum's Department of Greek and Roman Art, after a fellowship at the American Academy in Rome. There he had been in close touch with Miss Richter and knew of her investigation. The following supplementary reports by Miss Richter were addressed to Mr. Hoffmann, after his departure for New York. To a letter he sent on October 15, 1958, Miss Richter replied on October 18: "I have written to Riccardi since my return, but have as yet no answer. I hope he is investigating. At all events, that story of Ugo Jandolo's, of his having seen the warriors at Stettiner's (= a forger) is not correct, for I learned now also from Sangiorgi, who knew Stettiner well, that he was a high official at the Post Office and a *collector*, not a forger. So that is that. And, as I told you, that was the only thing I heard about the affair that ever disturbed me."

On October 21, 1958, Amedeo Riccardi finally wrote Miss Richter from Florence that the following week he was to meet the person who, he hoped, would furnish the desired information; he added that as soon as he had something precise, he would not fail to let her know. This was followed in May 1959 by a visit of Riccardi to Rome, at which time he showed Miss Richter a letter to him from a certain Menchinelli of Orvieto. In this letter (dated January 17, 1959), his informant reports that in his youth he saw many blocks of stone similar to volcanic lava, mixed with terracotta and clay slabs, etc., which the peasants transported to fill a big ditch. The place they were discovered could be found again, and Riccardi proposed to get a permit to make researches (*indagini*) in that zone, in the hope of finding some ancient fragments.

After this visit to Miss Richter, nothing else came from Amedeo Riccardi. She kept up a correspondence with him, but with attacks of influenza, the spring plowing, and the fields under cultivation, he was not able to help more. It looked as if we had come to a dead end.

A different investigation, this one limited to New

19. [See above, page 8, note 5. Now vindicated through the discovery of a similar sarcophagus at Vulci (C. M. Lerici *Alla Scoperta delle civiltà sepolte* [1960] pp. 366-69).]

York and the archives of the Museum, concerned the official vendor of the old warrior and the colossal head. He was Pietro Stettiner, already mentioned above in Miss Richter's reply to Herbert Hoffmann of October 18, 1958. Altogether, Mr. Marshall bought fifteen objects from Mr. Stettiner, between 1914 and 1920. Mr. Stettiner became well known in 1911 as the author of a book on Rome, *Roma nei suoi monumenti*. Mr. Marshall first met him on October 24, 1913, in Stettiner's house at 68, Via del Boschetto. In his diary for that day, Mr. Marshall wrote: "His bust of a goddess seemed to me false—Helbig[20] came: told him that I thought Stettiner's head false. Jacobsen[21] had, it seems, expressed doubts about it." This "bust of a goddess" may be identical with the *mezza figura di fanciulla in terra cotta epoca basso impero* which Mr. Marshall acquired from Mr. Stettiner in 1916 (Plate xx A).[22] If it is, we shall never know what made Mr. Marshall change his mind. Perhaps the terracotta warriors and their appearance at Mr. Stettiner's, as well as his other antiquities, helped to dispel the first, bad impression. In any event, the upper part of this life-size terracotta statue of a woman arrived in New York barely in time to be included in the first edition of Miss Richter's *Handbook of the Classical Collection*,[23] which appeared in December 1917. After careful examination of the piece sometime between 1917 and 1927, the bust was retired as a

forgery. It is no longer mentioned in the second edition of the *Handbook*, and the catalogue card is marked "FORGERY" in Miss Richter's handwriting.[24]

The recognition that an acquisition from a dealer is a forgery often leads to a re-examination of other objects from the same source. In this case, in addition to the old warrior and the colossal head, we already had under investigation a series of seven terracotta slabs with sea monsters (*kētē*), dolphins, scallops, and the like, bought from Mr. Stettiner in 1914.[25] These small slabs (see Plate xxii A) remained for many years without published parallels. In Mr. Marshall's list of purchases for 1914, they are said to come from Cervetri. In the receipt signed by Mr. Stettiner on June 4, 1914, they are merely called *terrecotte (sette pezzi) policromate etrusche*. They were immediately published in the Museum's *Bulletin*[26] and were described in the *Handbook* of 1917.[27] With the doubts centering around Mr. Stettiner, these plaques were cleaned in the winter of 1960/61 and soaked apart. It did not take long to unmask them as forgeries. The mistakes in the details of the dolphins (equipped with extra fins) and the poor rendering of the crests of the kētē, as well as the ill-defined scallops, came under the heading of stylistic grounds, but the more revealing and most conclusive arguments were produced by an examination of the technique. It was discovered that several of these plaques had been broken *before* firing. This was proved by the differing colors of the fragments and by the very nature of the breaks (some of which must have occurred while the clay was still wet). Moreover, some of the plaques had been painted after they had been broken, for in many instances the color of the background, a bluish slate gray, covered the fractures. A spectrographic analysis of the colors of one of the plaques (see Appendix C) revealed manganese and zinc as the coloring agents for the red, cobalt and lead for the bottom coat of the grayish blue, and cobalt as the coloring agent for the top layer of the blue. Thus, once again the coloring and the technique condemned the pieces.

The basic elements of the design on the reliefs were known in Etruscan art.[28] The composition was evidently based on a fragmentary frieze, found about 1880, in Orvieto (Plate xxii C, D)[29] and on fragments of another frieze, sold in 1909 to Copenhagen (see Plate xxii E).[30] The seven plaques in New York are not isolated. There are other replicas, taken from the same mold or prototype, in the Villa

---

20. [At that time the purchasing agent for the Ny Carlsberg Glyptotek in Copenhagen.]

21. [The founder of the Ny Carlsberg Glyptotek.]

22. Acc. no. 16.141. The Italian description of the bust is taken from the bill.

23. Seventh Room, Pedestal O, p. 167.

24. The necklace seems to have been copied from the drawing of a sarcophagus (now in Palermo) in G. Micali *Storia degli antichi popoli italiani* (1836) pl. 60 (Plate xxi B) and from such genuine Caeretan terracotta busts as New York 96.18.174 (Plate xxi A). As Edward Robinson saw (in *Thirteenth Annual Report* [Museum of Fine Arts, Boston, 1889] pp. 14-15), the jewelry of the Palermo sarcophagus also occurs on a terracotta bust (Plate xx B) once in Boston (acc. no. 88.537) and returned in 1906 to the donor, Mrs. H. D. Wilmarth. Professor H. R. W. Smith very kindly drew my attention to this bust, which had also fallen under suspicion.

25. Acc. no. 14.105.8 a-g.

26. X (1915) pp. 208, 210, fig. 2.

27. P. 166.

28. Cf. Vatican inv. 13844 (Plate xxii B); Arvid Andrén *Architectural Terracottas from Etrusco-Italic Temples* (1939-40) pp. 508-9, pl. 159, fig. 547.

29. Museo dell' Opera del Duomo; Andrén *op. cit.* p. 201, pl. 74, figs. 252-53.

30. Ny Carlsberg Glyptotek, I.N. 2464 (Plate xxii E) and T 148 a; Andrén *op. cit.* pl. 159, fig. 548. Now taken apart and cleaned.

Giulia and the Antiquarium of the Palazzo dei Conservatori in Rome, in the museum at Mannheim,[31] and in the market.[32] The New York slabs were said to be from Cervetri; the relief in the Marseilles market was said to be from Sicily; the one in Mannheim was bought in Rome; the other reliefs, in the museums of Rome and in the Signorelli collection, according to Signorelli, Fallani, and Colini, all came from the same source, Elio and Ugo Jandolo.

These marine monster plaques form part of a larger complex (see Plate XXIII), which includes five other types of architectural terracottas. The complex was first published by Colini,[33] discussed by Andrén,[34] and more of its history was given by Fallani in his sale catalogue of the Signorelli collection.[35] Colini supposed that the terracottas came from an Etruscan temple in the neighborhood of Bolsena. The first reliefs of the complex to be sold abroad were those acquired by the National Museum in Copenhagen in 1910;[36] Signorelli made his purchase between 1911 and 1916; the New York reliefs were bought in 1914.

Since the five other types of architectural terracottas are not represented in the Museum's collection, they could not be analyzed. The nature of the breaks and an examination of the surface, however, allow the provisional conclusion that all six types are false, made in the same workshop after 1910, probably in Orvieto.

This investigation brought us a step closer to understanding the origin of our terracotta warriors, for in spite of the difference in size, the warriors and the architectural plaques have much in common. To begin with, the reliefs and two of the statues were bought from Mr. Stettiner; they were fired in fragments, and they were colored with manganese. The reputed provenance of the reliefs, Bolsena, is not too far from the alleged site of the discovery of the warriors.

The connection between Mr. Stettiner and the Riccardis is not only implied in the correspondence, it can actually be proved through a receipt for two antiquities sold to Mr. Marshall, which was signed by Amedeo Riccardi and Pietro Stettiner on January 29, 1920. Mr. Stettiner must have died later in 1920 or shortly thereafter, for he no longer appears in the correspondence.

There remained a few other leads to be followed through. Professor Cagiano had told the writer in the winter of 1959 that he knew the man who made the warriors. A correspondence with Professor Cagiano was begun on October 26, 1960 and continued through January 1961. In February of 1953, he had come across in the Uffizio di Esportazione a terracotta statue in the Etruscan style which was being exported as modern. The shipper was asked to make a deposition, and he declared that it had been made in Orvieto in the workshop of the Riccardis. Further researches in Orvieto had led Cagiano to an old man who remembered having worked in his youth, during the First World War, in the Riccardi workshop and having been present at the construction of some gigantic Etruscan warriors which were sold abroad. In his first letter, Cagiano said he believed the old man to have died; later he discovered that he was still alive, and gave us his name in a letter of January 26, 1961. Professor Cagiano had shown photographs of the warriors to the old man, but his reply (transmitted by his son) was disappointing: he was not sure he had seen these statues in the Riccardis' workshop; he only remembered with certainty having seen the brothers construct an entire Roman biga.[37]

I had suspected that Professor Cagiano's informant would turn out to be the Fioravanti mentioned as early as 1936 as one of the collaborators on the New York warriors, but he was not. Fioravanti's name had come up again in a letter of February 17, 1958 from Harold W. Parsons to Mr.

---

31. Mentioned erroneously under Heidelberg by K. Shepard *The Fish-tailed Monster in Greek and Etruscan Art* (1940) p. 83, note 14, no. 8.

32. Marseilles (seen at O. Ravel's in 1948); Rome (G. Fallani *Raccolta archeologica del Prof. Dott. Angelo Signorelli* [1951] pp. 8, 26, nos. 119-23); and London (*Cat. Sotheby, 12 December 1960* p. 41, lot 145).

33. In *Studi etruschi* IX (1935) pp. 95 ff.

34. *Op. cit.* pp. 207 ff.

35. *Op. cit.* p. 26.

36. Niels Breitenstein *Catalogue of Terracottas* (1941) p. 82, no. 778, pl. 95.

37. Though not much was gained for the warriors, the statement connected the Riccardi workshop with the construction of a Roman biga that can be identified with the bronze chariot in the British Museum (1911.4-18.1). It was said to have been found in the district of Prodo, on the road from Orvieto to Todi, in December 1908 and was purchased from Domenico Fuschini of Orvieto. The records in the British Museum, kindly shown to me by D. E. L. Haynes, Keeper of Greek and Roman Antiquities, reveal that the chariot was restored by Pio Riccardi of Rome. Needless to say, the chariot is no longer on exhibition, having been recognized as a pasticcio many years ago. It was described in the Acquisitions Report of the British Museum in *Archaeologischer Anzeiger* (1912) col. 601, no. 12, and illustrated by C. K. Loukomski *L'Art étrusque* (1930) pl. 57. A similar chariot that appeared in the Roman market in 1947 was offered to The Metropolitan Museum of Art; it was not recommended for purchase, being recognized as inauthentic.

Rorimer, in which Mr. Parsons identified a certain Alfredo Fioravanti as the sculptor of a terracotta statue in the Ny Carlsberg Glyptotek, the well-known Copenhagen kore.[38] Although Mr. Parsons spoke in the same letter of the terracotta warriors as being false, he did not associate them with Alfredo Fioravanti. Mr. Parsons, who has lived in Rome since 1953, had communicated his doubts freely and frequently over the years. Visitors to his apartment in New York and later in Rome were usually shown albums and folders in which Mr. Parsons had assembled his collection of photographs of forgeries—some old and acknowledged, others denied by the owners, or, as in the case of the New York warriors, still under investigation. I had not seen Mr. Parsons since early 1953, but from time to time I received accounts from friends who had seen him. At a chance meeting with Professor Walter Cook, the former Head of the Department of Fine Arts of New York University, in early November of 1960, the subject of the Etruscan warriors came up; Professor Cook, having recently returned from Europe, reported that Mr. Parsons was working on them and was collecting evidence of their modern origin. Professor Cook volunteered to write Mr. Parsons and ask him whether he had any new details. On December 12, 1960, the latter wrote at length to Professor Cook, authorizing him to show us any part of the letter of interest to us, and Professor Cook did so on January 10, 1961. The most important piece of new evidence was Mr. Parsons's revelation that he had recently seen the missing left thumb of the big warrior, which had been kept as a souvenir by one of its creators, who was still alive. In the meantime, Mr. Rorimer had written Mr. Parsons on December 16, 1960 and asked whether he had unearthed any facts that further confirmed his opinion about the authenticity of the warriors. A reply to this letter arrived January 12, and Mr. Parsons enclosed a translation of a deposition signed by Alfredo Adolfo Fioravanti before the American Consul in Rome on January 5, 1961. In it Fioravanti confirmed the story told twenty-five years before, that he had helped to make the three terracotta warriors in the Metropolitan Museum. He not only owned the left thumb of the big warrior (see Plate XIX) but also two test pieces of terracotta with the black glaze and the accessory colors (Plate XVIII), as well as bits of unfired clay similar to that used in the body of the big warrior and the colossal head.

My visit to Rome from February 6 to 12 of 1961 brought about two talks with Fioravanti, kindly arranged by Mr. Parsons; I was able to conclude the investigation, not only through these interviews, but also through several meetings with Miss Richter, Professor Pallottino, and Professor Cagiano, and finally through a visit to Orvieto. The following account is in part taken from the detailed report by Mr. Parsons to Mr. Rorimer, corroborated through the conversations with Alfredo Adolfo Fioravanti, and checked in details through talks with others.

It should be pointed out that the possession of the missing thumb was in itself no proof that the owner was also the maker of the statue. Since the big warrior had been acquired in many fragments, a piece of it could well have been lost or purposely retained by any one of the many people connected with the so-called excavation, the transport, the packing, and the shipping.[39] By the same token the test tiles merely confirmed what had already been proved, namely, that the statues were modern. What was needed to establish the credibility of Fioravanti was his affirmation of facts not previously known or said concerning the manufacture of the statues, and, if possible, the verification of his suspected participation in other works.

The results of the direct interviews were most revealing. The spectrographic tests made in January of 1960 had already shown us that the color of the glaze was achieved with manganese dioxide. Fioravanti at once volunteered the information that the glaze was *biossido di manganese* and added that it had been bought in Milan. The use of manganese in a modern workshop in Orvieto is understandable, since it is a common coloring agent in modern ceramic glazes and was thought to have been an ingredient of ancient *bucchero*.[40] In this case, however,

---

38. H.I.N. 476 (H 845). The first account is that of Frederik Poulsen in *Die Antike* VIII (1932) pp. 95-104, figs. 1-6, pls. 13-15; the statue was republished fully by P. J. Riis *From the Collections of the Ny Carlsberg Glyptothek* III (1942) pp. 1-10, figs. 1-5. Spectrographic analyses of the glaze and clay body are given in Appendix C.

39. Or it could have been suppressed for aesthetic reasons: the photograph of the left hand with the thumb attached (see Plate XIX) shows how inelegant it looks.

40. Cf. A. del Vita "Osservazioni sulla tecnologia del bucchero" in *Studi etruschi* I (1927) pp. 187 ff. and the explanation of *bucchero* on a label in the Museo Nazionale in Palermo, *di argilla impastata con minerale manganese e cotta all' aperto*, observed and kindly copied out for me by K. Lefferts, Assistant Conservator in The Metropolitan Museum of Art. This explanation is included in Delia Lollini's account of *bucchero* in *Enciclopedia dell' arte antica* II (1959) pp. 203 ff. For the correct solution see Miss Richter's "The Technique of Bucchero Ware" in *Studi etruschi* X (1936) p. 62.

it becomes especially significant. We knew that an older generation of Riccardis had worked for Domenico Fuschini, the vendor of the forged Roman biga to the British Museum,[41] and Mr. Parsons's researches also established a connection between Fuschini and the trade in Orvieto-ware maiolica,[42] of which manganese is the chief coloring agent. The production of this forged maiolica had begun quite innocently with the repair of maiolica vases found in great quantities in fragments in the abandoned wells of Orvieto, had graduated from there to the restoration of missing pieces, and finally culminated in the manufacture of complete vases, skillfully broken before firing. Fuschini probably first met the brothers Pio and Alfonso Riccardi in Rome, where they had established a workshop when they left their ancestral home in Trevi del Lazio, near Assisi, after their father's death in a cholera epidemic; Pio "repaired" the Roman biga there at Fuschini's request. Later Fuschini must have found it more convenient to have him move with his family to Orvieto; it was there, in any event, that Pio died in 1912. He had four sons, Riccardo, Amedeo, Gino, and Fausto; his brother Alfonso had two, Teodoro and Virgilio Angelino.

Fioravanti said he had collaborated in the creation of the terracotta warriors with three Riccardis: Riccardo and his cousins Teodoro and Virgilio Angelino, all of whom are now dead. Riccardo, the eldest, was born in 1886; during the winter of 1918/19, he was thrown from a horse and killed instantly. He was the "capable" one mentioned by Professor Curtis on August 1, 1919. One report has it that Teodoro posed for the big warrior. Teodoro, who sold Mr. Marshall objects in 1925 and 1926, had no fixed residence, living now in Orvieto and now in Siena; he has also been traced to Terni. He and his brother Virgilio were exempt from military service during the First World War as *mezzo matto*, and one of the two must be the "half-crazy" brother mentioned in the Marshall correspondence. Fioravanti was the special friend of Riccardo Riccardi, and one gathers that after his death there was a general falling out between his cousins and Fioravanti.

Fioravanti also remembered his beginnings in the Riccardis' workshop in the days of their connection with Domenico Fuschini. He acknowledged having made the terracotta slabs with sea monsters (including the seven in this Museum); he also mentioned of his own accord the other types of that complex and remembered that they had been sold to Elio and Ugo Jandolo. His detailed account of how molds were made of pieces in Orvieto and then elaborated not only explains the difference in size between the originals and the modern pieces; it also establishes his presence in Orvieto and his connection with the Riccardis at least as early as 1914, the date when the seven New York slabs were sold through Mr. Stettiner.

One of the questions which everybody wished to see answered was, of course, that of the prototypes or models for the Etruscan warriors. Miss Richter, in her account in the "Papers,"[43] had already recognized the similarity between the big warrior and a small bronze statuette from Dodona in Berlin (Plate XVII).[44] Pallottino, it will be remembered, went one step further in his article of 1937[45] and claimed this Dodona bronze to be the prototype of the big warrior. The Dodona bronze had been known through casts and illustrations since 1881, and a bronze copy of it was made a long time ago in Rome by del Nero. According to Fioravanti, the del Nero copy was not used, but merely a tiny reproduction of the Dodona bronze in a popular picture book.[46] For the ornaments, Fioravanti tells me that the Riccardis consulted a great many books and photographs, as well as objects in Orvieto.[47] Pallottino was also right in a second assumption, namely, that the colossal head was inspired by the small East Greek vases in the shape of helmeted heads.[48] Many such vases were found in Etruria and they were, therefore, considered Etruscan by some Italians. Fioravanti admitted that these small vases served as models, calling them, understandably, Etruscan. It is no mere coincidence that Teodoro Riccardi sold two vases in the shape of helmeted heads (Plate VII B, C) to Mr. Marshall in 1921.[49]

41. See above, p. 15, note 37.

42. Cf. the charming account by Augusto Jandolo in *Le Memorie di un antiquario* (2nd ed., 1938) pp. 146 ff.

43. P. 10, notes 20-21, pl. III B.

44. Inv. 7470; K. A. Neugebauer *Die griechischen Bronzen der klassischen Zeit und des Hellenismus* (1951) p. 57 (with complete bibliography).

45. In *Roma* (1937) p. 474.

46. Emanuel Löwy *Die griechische Plastik* (Leipzig, 1911) pl. 12, fig. 31.

47. Several of the patterns on the big warrior appear in Paul R. Bollo's line drawings of the Monteleone chariot in New York (acc. no. 03.23.1; found in 1902 and first published in 1904); the drawings (see Plate XVI) are reproduced in Miss Richter's publication of the chariot in *Greek, Etruscan and Roman Bronzes* (1915) pp. 17-29. Mr. Bollo was the Museum's draftsman from 1893 to 1935.

48. Most examples of this type are collected and discussed by J. Ducat in *Revue des études anciennes* LIX (1957) pp. 233 ff.

49. Acc. nos. 21.88.170 and 21.88.171.

Another possible source of inspiration was mentioned by Professor Cagiano, who thinks that the big stone head of a helmeted warrior in the Museo dell' Opera del Duomo in Orvieto[50] could also have been used in the planning of the colossal head.

For the earliest purchase, the old warrior, no single prototype has come to light. The statue reminded Mr. Parsons of the reclining man on the (false) Castellani sarcophagus in the British Museum.[51] But there are other possibilities. Mr. Marshall, in his very first letter about this terracotta (November 14, 1915), compared it to an elegant bronze statuette in Florence.[52] Our warrior's emaciated form and the shape of his helmet and crest are even closer to the Italic bronze statuettes from the Etruscan hinterland, of which there are many examples in the museums of the world.[53] In most of these Italic examples, the warriors are young men. They wear greaves, an "Attic" helmet with turned-up cheekpieces, and a leather or linen corselet, often with *pteryges* (lappets). The right arm is usually raised, with the fist drilled for the insertion of a spear. In a more primitive variety of this type, both arms hang rather loosely down, with the hands pierced for weapons,[54] and there is less detail in dress and armor.

There are several bronze statuettes of this type in The Metropolitan Museum of Art, but only one of them was acquired by Mr. Marshall. On April 15, 1919, he obtained from Mr. Stettiner an exceptionally large statuette (Plates IV-V), which since its purchase has frequently been published and illustrated.[55] Apart from its size (10⅝ inches), the statuette exhibited several peculiarities which have not been noted before. The warrior was *bearded*; his hands were open, not pierced; the helmet was of the *Corinthian* type; his cuirass appeared to be of *metal* and was decorated with two spirals around the breasts, a lanceolate pattern around the neck, and multiple engraved horizontal bands along the lower edge. The proportions of the figure, however, were those of the more primitive type, in which the armor is less sophisticated. The answer to these puzzling incongruities has been provided by cleaning (Plates IV and V B, C). The so-called patina turned out to be largely paint, wax, and gesso and yielded readily, and the new photographs show what the statuette really is—a pasticcio. The crest is an alien piece of bronze, reworked and inserted; the head is completely reworked, with the mouth, beard, nosepiece, and part of the cheekpieces added in bronze, and the rest recut to conform with the desired shape. The neckline of the cuirass and the double lines setting off the arms from the body are likewise modern, as are the contour lines of the greaves. The volutes on the chest disappeared in the cleaning and gave way to two plain circles for the nipples. The lanceolate pattern around the neck is much fainter than before and is no longer part of the cuirass. In fact, the cuirass too has vanished, and it turns out that the statuette is a most extraordinary assembly of the upper part of a *woman* (hence the arms without weapons or armor) joined to the lower part of a *man*. The figure was elongated by the addition of a bronze mid-section, attached with a copper rivet, and by extra lengths of shanks in brass; it was transformed into a warrior by the rechasing of the head, the contouring of the shanks for greaves, the addition of nosepiece, beard, and cheekpieces, and the insertion of a crest.

This weird creation, it seems, could only have served one purpose: it was meant to unite the various unusual features of the terracotta sculptures, namely, the elongated proportions (like those of Italic statuettes) of the old warrior, who wears an "Attic" helmet with turned-up cheekpieces but a *metal* cuirass, and the *Corinthian* helmet of the colossal bearded head. In the absence of documentary proof, it is hard to establish the exact date when the bronze statuette was assembled. One small detail, however, may indicate an approximate date. The underside of the beard of the colossal head is flat, although it would have been visible if the head were shown on a high pedestal or if it had surmounted a statue. The beard of the big warrior, on the other hand, is treated in detail both on the top surface and on the underside (see Plate XV B). The sculptural detail is precisely the same on both sides of the

50. Ugo Tarchi *L'Arte etrusco-romana nell' Umbria e nella Sabina* (1936) pl. 61, upper right.

51. B 630 (1873.8-20.643); G. Q. Giglioli *L'Arte etrusca* (1935) p. 24, pl. 116,1; Herta Sauer *Die archaischen etruskischen Terracottasarkophage aus Caere* (1930) pp. 42 ff., pl. 2,1.

52. L. A. Milani *Il R. Museo Archeologico di Firenze* Vol. II (Atlante) pl. 30; Giglioli *op. cit.* p. 24, pl. 120,1; L. Goldscheider *Etruscan Sculpture* (1941) pl. 107.

53. Cf. G. Bendinelli in *Monumenti antichi* XXVI (1920) pp. 221-46; Giglioli *op. cit.* p. 40, pls. 221,3 – 222, 1-4; Doro Levi in *Record of the Museum of Historic Art, Princeton University* (1942) pp. 9-13; E. Hill "Etruscan Votive Bronze Warriors" in *Journal of the Walters Art Gallery* VI-VII (1944-45) pp. 104-24; *eadem* in *Memoirs of the American Academy at Rome* XXI (1953) pp. 99-100.

54. Cf. Giglioli *op. cit.* pl. 222, no. 6.

55. Acc. no. 19.192.2. *The Metropolitan Museum of Art Bulletin* XVI (1921) pp. 35-36; *Master Bronzes* (Buffalo Fine Arts Academy, 1937) no. 80 (ill.); Goldscheider *op. cit.* pl. 77.

beard of the bronze statuette, and it would therefore be perfectly proper archaeological procedure to date the manufacture of the bronze statuette after the creation of the colossal head and either before or contemporary with the big warrior.

According to Fioravanti, the old warrior and the colossal head were finished before he and Riccardo Riccardi went into the army. They were made and fired in the old Riccardi shop in the Via San Paolo in Orvieto. The old warrior exhibits two peculiarities which have always puzzled us: he has no right arm, though otherwise remarkably complete, and the walls of his trunk are so thin in places (see Plate II A, B) that a crack developed after the statue had come to New York. Fioravanti's revelations explain both points. It seems that the sculptors of the warrior could not agree on the position of the right arm, and it was therefore simply never fired. As to the thin wall of the trunk, Fioravanti claims that he warned the Riccardis against scraping away too much of the surface in modeling the figure, since he realized that the walls would become too thin.

It must have been immediately after the armistice of 1918 that work was begun on the big warrior. Both Fioravanti and Riccardo Riccardi had served in the same regiment in the Italian army and were demobilized at the same time, and Fioravanti remembers that Riccardo Riccardi died at a time when the big warrior was not yet finished. His death, in the winter of 1918/19, perhaps explains why the big warrior was the last large-scale terracotta created by the group in Orvieto. Fioravanti asserts that this warrior was made in a small room on the ground floor of a rented house in the Via dei Magoni at Orvieto, and gives an honest explanation of the statue's stocky proportions. The warrior was being built from the ground up, but by the time the waist had been reached, it became obvious that the elegant proportions of the Dodona warrior, its model, could not be kept because the ceiling was too low. Adjustments had to be made from the waist up, and these account for its stocky

build. The difficulty of judging the proportions also explains the overlong left arm: there was no possibility of stepping far enough back to judge the results from a decent distance. Moreover, the lower part of the body was mostly hidden by the moist rags wrapped around it and by the many sticks and slats which formed a scaffolding, so the relation of the arm to the rest of the statue could not be judged. The glaze and colored decoration were applied while the warrior was still in one piece; the supports were shifted during this operation. Afterwards, it was allowed to crack in the drying and was pushed to the floor, so that it broke into many fragments. Originally the plinth on which the warrior stands was much bigger, but Fioravanti tells me that only part of the plinth was fired; the rest was thrown away.

The firing of the big warrior, in several batches of broken pieces, took two nights and one day. The kilns for this and the other warriors were of the traditional Orvieto type; not more than four feet in height and about three feet deep and less than three feet wide. In these kilns, of which I saw one of the few still left in Orvieto, there are no doors; the whole front of the kiln is open and is bricked up for the firing. The fuel is wood, and the right temperature—about 900° C.—is judged by looking through a peephole at the color of the kiln and by drawpieces attached to long iron pokers.

There are, no doubt, other details of the creation and construction of the Museum's warriors which Fioravanti either does not know or does not remember. They become, of course, somewhat academic when compared with the chief question, that of the age of the warriors. From this point of view, the investigation can now be considered concluded, since we have not only scientific proof that the construction and the glaze of the warriors fail to conform to ancient practices and must be modern, but also the sworn testimony of Alfredo Adolfo Fioravanti of Rome, whose participation in the creation of the warriors has been established.

PROOF OF THE FORGERY:
TECHNICAL CONSIDERATIONS

by Joseph V. Noble

FROM THE TIME of their acquisition by The Metropolitan Museum of Art, in 1915, 1916, and 1921, the three monumental terracotta warriors (see Plates I, VI, X) were subjected to prolonged examination to determine the techniques used in their manufacture. The first technical studies were undertaken by Charles F. Binns, Director of the New York State School of Clay-working and Ceramics at Alfred University (Alfred, New York), who was retained by the Museum for this purpose. They were also thoroughly examined by Edward Robinson, Director of the Museum and Curator of Classical Art, and Gisela M. A. Richter, his Associate Curator at that time. Mr. Binns's report on the structure and technique of the big warrior is incorporated in Miss Richter's publication of the terracottas in the Metropolitan Museum "Papers,"[1] which appeared after his death; the final report also includes observations by the late Maude Robinson, a potter and ceramic expert of New York City.

Binns stated that the terracotta was composed of clay mixed with sand and grog (fired, crushed pottery) to minimize shrinkage and that the figures were built up in sections using rolls or wads of clay. From his examination of the inside surfaces of the fragments of the figures before they were put together for exhibition, he was able to ascertain that they were modeled freehand, not poured or pressed into molds (see Plate XV). He thought that during the construction the figures were supported by wooden props, and after drying fired *in situ*, pointing out that any attempt to move them in the unfired state would surely have resulted in their cracking and collapsing. The kiln would have been built over the figures. He estimated that several months would probably have been required for a firing at 960° C.

and the subsequent slow cooling to prevent breakage.

It had been assumed by Mr. Robinson, Miss Richter, and Mr. Binns that the black glaze that covered all three statues was similar to the ancient Greek black glaze used on Attic, Etruscan, and other classical vases.

From time to time, questions about the authenticity of these figures were raised, both on stylistic and on technical grounds. The details of this controversy, together with the history of the acquisition of the warriors, are documented here in the section by Dietrich von Bothmer. Obviously, definitive and incontrovertible evidence was needed either to prove or disprove the authenticity of the figures.

During 1958 I became interested in the practical applications of the late Theodor Schumann's explanation of the ancient method of producing the Greek black glaze. Dr. Schumann had discovered that the ancient black glaze was made from the same red clay as the body of Greek vases, with no coloring agents added to achieve the black color.[2] He reproduced it by using a peptized clay slip as the glaze matter and subjecting his pottery to oxidizing, reducing, and reoxidizing firing conditions.

The chemistry of the process is as follows. Red ferric oxide (Fe_2O_3) is present both in the clay body of the vase and in the unfired black glaze matter, which is made from the clay by a deflocculating separation process that extracts only the finest particles of the clay. The particles, mixed with water, are used as a slip for the decoration of the vase. If the entire firing were done under oxidizing conditions (in which air is allowed to enter the kiln), both the vase and the glaze would turn, and remain, red.

In the middle of the firing cycle, however, the oxidizing atmosphere is changed to a reducing atmosphere by the introduction of green wood or damp sawdust. The smoke produced by this action is not important chemically as it is largely composed of carbon, which does not affect the coloring of the black glaze. The reducing atmosphere, with the kiln closed to the outside supply of oxygen, causes incomplete combustion of the green wood or wet sawdust and produces carbon monoxide gas (CO), instead of the carbon dioxide gas (CO_2) which

---

1. Gisela M. A. Richter *Etruscan Terracotta Warriors in The Metropolitan Museum of Art*, "Papers" No. 6 (The Metropolitan Museum of Art, 1937).

2. "Oberflächenverzierung in der antiken Töpferkunst. Terra sigillata und griechische Schwarzrotmalerei" in *Berichte der deutschen keramischen Gesellschaft* XXIII (1942) pp. 408-26 (summarized by C. Weickert "Zur Technik der griechischen Vasenmalerei" in *Archaeologischer Anzeiger* [1942] cols. 512-28) and "Terra sigillata und die Schwarz-Rot-Malerei der Griechen" in *Forschungen und Fortschritte* XIX (1943) pp. 356-58. His findings did not become available outside continental Europe until after 1945.

would be developed during normal, complete combustion. Carbon monoxide unites with any oxygen that it can obtain. In this case it combines with part of the oxygen in the ferric oxide (Fe_2O_3) of the clay. This changes part of the carbon monoxide into the stable form, carbon dioxide, and the red *ferric* oxide (Fe_2O_3) into *ferrous* oxide (FeO), which is black. The reaction in this process is $Fe_2O_3 + CO = 2FeO + CO_2$. Water vapor in the kiln, from the moisture of the pottery, from the green wood or wet sawdust, or perhaps even from a vessel filled with water in the kiln itself, also produces a black glaze, a magnetic oxide of iron (Fe_3O_4), which is even blacker than mere ferrous oxide (FeO). The reaction in this process is $3Fe_2O_3 + CO = 2Fe_3O_4 + CO_2$. If the firing cycle were stopped at this point, the clay body of the vase and the glaze would be completely and permanently black.

The process is concluded by a reoxidizing phase. Through a small hole now opened, oxygen is again permitted to enter the kiln; it unites with some of the black ferrous oxide (FeO) or magnetic oxide of iron (Fe_3O_4), turning it back into the red ferric oxide (Fe_2O_3). The porous clay body of the vase readily allows this to happen, and consequently unglazed portions of the surface and most of the body again turn red. On the other hand, the glazed areas have sintered and do not reoxidize at the temperature of this last phase, which does not exceed 1000° C. These areas remain black, and the result of the three-phase firing is the red and black coloring characteristic of ancient, especially Attic, vases.

That this was the ancient Greek and Etruscan technique of making black glaze can be scientifically confirmed. Spectrographic analyses of the body and the glaze of genuine classical pottery are identical, except for a slightly greater concentration of the heavier minerals in the glaze. They do not show any added coloring agent in the black glaze. The spectrographic method is, therefore, an excellent way to differentiate between genuine ancient vases and imitations.

This test would prove at once whether the fired black glaze of the warriors was indeed an ancient one, as Miss Richter and Mr. Binns had assumed.[3] If it were proved that the black glaze was not identical to the ancient glaze, but included an added coloring agent, then it was certain that the figures were forgeries.

In January 1960, spectrographic analyses of the clay body and the glaze of the three warriors were made for the Museum by Lucius Pitkin, Inc., a technical laboratory in New York City. For comparative purposes, analyses were also made of an Etruscan architectural tile[4] that was known to be genuine. The spectrographic analyses (see Appendices A and B) revealed that in the tile there was only a trace of manganese present in the glaze, whereas in the black glaze of the three warriors there were very substantial amounts of manganese. The disproportionate amount of manganese indicated that it had been added to the glaze of the three warriors as a coloring agent. The use of manganese in a ceramic glaze was, of course, known in ancient Egypt and the ancient Near East, but it was not employed in Greece in classical times. Manganese was not used in Italy until the introduction of the manufacture of maiolica, of which it is one of the chief coloring agents. In modern times it was used for the reproduction of *bucchero* vases in the workshop of Alessandro and Antonio del Vita, and it was even assumed in Italy that ancient *bucchero* was made with manganese. We already knew, through spectrographic analysis (see Appendix C), that one of the two Tarquinia imitators of Attic and Etruscan pottery, Scapini, employed cobalt, lead, and manganese as coloring agents for his excellent reproductions of the Greek black glaze.

The old warrior does not have any more manganese in the clay body than the amount normally present in most central Italian clays, Etruscan or modern; the amount is identical, in fact, to that in the Etruscan architectural tile. Therefore, in the old warrior the concentration of manganese in the

---

3. On December 29, 1959, I read a paper entitled "The Technique of Attic Vase-Painting" at the general meeting of the Archaeological Institute of America held in New York City. As part of that report, I described the test of the comparative analysis to differentiate between genuine Attic vases and modern imitations. In addition, I pointed out, "This test is also applicable to terracotta figures or other objects decorated with black glaze which were known before the discoveries of Schumann in 1942." The paper was later published in the *American Journal of Archaeology* LXIV (1960) pp. 307-18, pls. 84-87 and color plate.

4. Acc. no. X. 379. This is one of three Etruscan architectural terracottas which had been in the storerooms of the Greek and Roman Department for many years. The pieces are not mentioned or described in any of the lists of collections or purchases before 1906. It is possible, though this cannot be proved, that they were included in the shipment of one of the warriors. In his letter of August 3, 1917, Mr. Marshall mentions "large tiles coming from a big temple" as allegedly found with the old warrior and the colossal head; perhaps the vendors let him have these three architectural fragments, which may be stray finds from the region of Orvieto. The only parallel for one of them was supplied by Arvid Andrén in a letter: he compares the cover tile X. 380 with Orvieto, Museo dell' Opera del Duomo, 2030 (p. 170, no. I,3 [not illustrated] in his *Architectural Terracottas from Etrusco-Italic Temples* [1939-40]).

21

black glaze differs from the amount present in the clay body. The colossal head and the big warrior, however, have manganese also added to the clay. This was probably done to darken the color of the terracotta to imitate the gray color of the interior of fractures of ancient terracotta pieces that had been subjected to a three-stage firing, or to copy *bucchero* ware. The series of spectrographic analyses, therefore, proved that the warriors were not made by a procedure known in classical antiquity.

To check this conclusion, an additional test was devised. Genuine ancient black glaze does not survive a temperature much above 1025° C., for at that temperature the black ferrous oxide begins to reoxidize to red ferric oxide and the black color is lost. On the other hand, a glaze made with a ceramic coloring agent, such as manganese, cobalt, or lead, will remain black at this temperature. A specimen of the glaze of the Etruscan architectural tile was heated to 1050° C.: the black reoxidized and became permanently red. This proved that this Etruscan glaze was similar in structure to Attic black glaze. Samples of the black glaze of the three warriors were subjected to the same 1050° C. temperature, and they remained black and unchanged. This second test gave corroborative proof that the glaze of the three warriors was not made by the ancient technique.

The next step, in order to draw the net tighter, was to ascertain the composition of the glaze of large-scale Etruscan or so-called Etruscan terracottas abroad. Spectrographic analyses (see Appendix C) of a specimen of the Castellani sarcophagus in the British Museum, an acknowledged forgery, revealed that the coloring agent was lead, whereas analyses of samples from genuine Caeretan slabs in the British Museum and in the Louvre (see Appendix A) agreed with those of the architectural terracotta in New York. Owing to a reorganization of the Villa Giulia in Rome, requests for samples from the Veii terracottas were not answered immediately, but when the specimens were obtained, they, too, confirmed the assumption that the glaze of large-scale Etruscan terracottas was achieved in exactly the same manner as the famous Greek glaze (see Appendix A).

An examination of the edges of breaks in the

warriors revealed that the clay body is uniform in color all the way through, indicating that the statues were fired only under oxidizing conditions. Pottery fired under the three-stage firing conditions usually is grayish in the core of the terracotta and reddish near the outside.

In addition to the warriors' black glaze and the uniform color of the terracotta, other clues pointed to their modern origin. Most important was the problem of their construction. Mr. Binns and Miss Robinson had concluded that each of the warriors had been fired in one piece, an extraordinary technical feat, and most of their researches had been centered on a practical explanation of this phenomenon. Unlike modern large-scale terracottas, such as the pedimental figures of the Philadelphia Museum of Art, the warriors had not been made in sections; the individual pieces in which they arrived were clearly broken (see Plates III, VIII, XII), not made separately and then keyed in. As the fragments fitted admirably together, it was naturally argued that they must have been broken *after* firing. Mr. Cellini stated, on the other hand, that the terracottas were fired in fragments[5] but did not give his reasons for saying so.

Now it must be remembered that at the time of the first purchase, that of the old warrior, the only comparable Etruscan terracottas on this scale were the Caeretan sarcophagi in the Villa Giulia and in the Louvre[6] and the (questioned) Castellani sarcophagus in the British Museum. The famous terracotta statues from Veii were not discovered until May 19, 1916 and were not published until 1919.[7] Curiously enough, none of the publications of ancient large-scale terracottas, not even the latest monograph on the three sarcophagi by Herta Sauer,[8] goes very thoroughly into the technical aspects of the construction, and we look in vain for a single reference to the construction of the Castellani sarcophagus. During the summer of 1960, Mr. von Bothmer and I examined separately all the large-scale terracotta statues in Cyprus, Greece, Italy, France, England, and Denmark. Our study disclosed the importance of ventholes, which allow an adequate circulation of air through the clay during drying and firing, in the construction of terracottas in antiquity. In large-scale Cypriot terracottas, there always is a profusion of ventholes, generally fairly large in size, often (as in Tarentine terracottas of smaller scale and later date) hidden by the insertion of a plug, fired separately and inserted later, with the edges concealed by unfired clay. Cypriot terra-

---

5. *Basti dire che fu necessario cuocerli a frammenti* (in *Paragone* LXV [1955] p. 46). See above, page 12, note 16.

6. Inv. Campana 5194 (see Plate XXIV).

7. G. Q. Giglioli in *Notizie degli scavi di antichità* pp. 13-37.

8. *Die archaischen etruskischen Terracottasarkophage aus Caere* (1930).

cottas are not very daring and are often made in pieces, joined after firing (as in modern practice). Greek terracottas, especially the biggish figures from Olympia[9] and Corinth,[10] display an amazing understanding of the problem of the ventilation of the clay. Semicircular or round holes on the front edge of the plinth allow access of the air, which then travels through the hollow parts of the sculptures. The most complete example of this construction in Greece is furnished by the group of Zeus and Ganymede in Olympia.[11] The torso of a striding heroic warrior,[12] also in Olympia, was constructed and fired in the same manner: an unattached fragment of his hollow left leg[13] is connected to the wing of a half-fallen opponent (perhaps, as Yalouris surmised, a gorgon) and through the latter with the plinth. The right leg with its solid ankle and foot did not require a separate air connection with the plinth, and the structural support was furnished, as in the Corinth pedimental group, through the fallen or falling figure.

Of the Olympia terracottas, only the head of Athena has a venthole on top of the head; it is in the helmet, cleverly concealed afterwards through the attachment of a separately fired crest.[14] According to Professor Kunze,[15] the group of Zeus and Ganymede has no ventholes in the *figures*; evidently the openings in the plinth sufficed for the intake and circulation of air. The terracotta head of a sphinx from Thebes, now in the Louvre,[16] has a large venthole on top of the head,[17] which would have been invisible to the spectator in antiquity. Ventholes of varying shapes and sizes are, of course, familiar to everybody from the backs of Tanagra statuettes.

As we turn to Etruria, we observe that in spite of differences in style and clay, the system of ventilation was the same as in Greece. The striding Apollo in the Villa Giulia is constructed like a chimney, with big holes for the intake of air between his legs and a large opening in his back, between his shoulder blades. The lid of the Caeretan sarcophagus in the Louvre[18] is detachable and hollow; it could have been fired upside down, without any ventholes, but even here adequate provision has been made for the air to escape (see Plate XXIV): the ears of both figures are pierced through (as they are on Cypriot terracottas and the sarcophagus in the Villa Giulia), the corners of the wineskin which serves as a cushion are likewise open, and even the thumbs have holes in them to allow an easy flow of air through the hollow arms and hands.

This provision for the ventilation of the clay in authentic Greek, Cypriot, and Etruscan terracottas is at variance with the technique employed for the warriors in New York. In the old warrior, only the trunk and thighs are hollow (see Plate II A, B) and there is no venthole. Since there was no possible way for the air to escape, the statue would have exploded had it been fired in one piece. It had been assumed, however, that there must have been a hole on top of the helmet, that was later covered by the crest (an assumption inconsistent with the hypothesis that the statue had been fired whole). The colossal head shows an improvement in technique in that it has one small venthole, about an inch in diameter, placed high on the helmet, next to the crest. The big warrior combines the half-hollow construction of the old warrior with the improvement of the venthole on top (Plate XV C). Although theoretically the single venthole might have been adequate for the ventilation of the colossal head, it would not have sufficed for the big warrior. Without an adequate circulation of air through the clay mass, the figures could not have dried properly before firing without incurring drying cracks (Plate XV D), which would have substantially weakened them. They could not have withstood the heat during firing with the resulting expansion and contraction of the clay and would not have remained whole. Thus, technically and historically, the lack of ventholes made it improbable that the warriors had been fired in one piece.

9. For the latest account, with a full bibliography, see E. Kunze in *Olympiabericht* VI (1958) pp. 169 ff.

10. Saul S. Weinberg "Terracotta Sculpture at Corinth" in *Hesperia* XXVI (1957) pp. 289-319, pls. 64-75.

11. *Olympiabericht* V (1956) pp. 103 ff.

12. *Ibid.* pp. 114 ff.

13. *Olympiabericht* III (1941) pl. 57, left.

14. *Olympiabericht* VI (1958) pp. 169 ff. The pair of ventholes on each cheek of the terracotta head of a warrior found in the Agora also served as rivet holes for the separately fired cheekpieces which are now missing. The head was published by Homer A. Thompson "Excavations in the Athenian Agora: 1953" in *Hesperia* XXIII (1954) pp. 61-62, pl. 14 a. Two holes on the right shoulder of the warrior from Olympia (above and below the baldric) may also have had a twofold purpose: to serve as ventholes and as dowel holes for the crest of the helmet. They are visible on plate 66 of *Olympiabericht* V (1956).

15. As reported to Bothmer in a letter of April 25, 1961.

16. Simone Mollard-Besques *Catalogue raisonné des figurines et reliefs en terre-cuite grecs, étrusques et romains* Vol. I (1954) pl. 17, no. B 131.

17. Not noted in the catalogue or the older publications, but visible in the line drawing of E. Pottier's article in *Monuments Piot* VI (1899) p. 140, fig. 3. Compare also the big venthole on top of the head of the sphinx from Calydon (E. Dyggve *Das Laphrion* [1948] pl. 22H, pp. 186-88, figs. 191-94).

18. Inv. Campana 5194.

There was also the question of how these enormous figures could have been supported during the firing. The big warrior weighed 800 pounds when it arrived at the Museum in a fragmentary condition, and the weight would have been 20 to 30 per cent greater before it was fired.

A new examination showed that the fit of the fragments was not so perfect as had been thought. Certain fractured areas, such as the locks of hair falling over the front of the neck of the big warrior (see Plate xiv), do not properly join; where this would have been obvious, the edges of the break have been chipped away to hide the telltale flaws. This suggested that the figures had warped and cracked in drying and probably were already in fragments before firing.

Subsequent to these investigations, Alfredo Adolfo Fioravanti, the last living member of the group that had created these forgeries, was located. In his interviews with Mr. von Bothmer in Rome, he corroborated all of our conclusions. He stated that the coloring agent was manganese dioxide, that the figures had been broken in many pieces before firing, and that the pieces were fired in relatively small kilns.

Fioravanti put at our disposal two fired terracotta test pieces (Plate xviii), which showed the black glaze and the clay slips used to decorate the figures. A spectrographic analysis of the clay of one of these test pieces shows the same concentration of added manganese found in the clay body of the colossal head and the big warrior. These test pieces were made after the manufacture of the old warrior, the clay body of which is a terracotta red and does not have the added manganese. The white and red slips used on the warriors were applied before firing. They lack a good clay binder and consequently are quite friable and in some instances rather powdery. As a result, the colors appear unfired or water soluble, though this is not the case. The colors are in the same friable condition on the test pieces. It is interesting to note that on one of the test pieces a light tan slip was tested, which, however, was not employed on the warriors.

One of the most useful pieces carefully kept by Fioravanti over the years was a specimen of unfired clay, similar to the clay body of the colossal head and the big warrior. This clay mixture contained grog and coarse sand and was colored by the addition of manganese (see Appendix B). In the unfired state, it is the color of dark mud. As a test, different fragments of the hunk of clay were fired to temperatures of 800° C., 900° C., and 1050° C. As the temperature increased, the intensity of the black color also increased. From the hardness of the terracotta of the warriors and from the color of their clay bodies, I estimate that the firing temperature of the figures was between 800° and 900° C. Probably the temperature varied during the different firings in the small kiln, for there are slight variations in the clay body color between some fragments of the same statue.

After samples of the unfired clay were fired, the results explained why the individually fired fragments of the warriors still joined almost perfectly: there had been very little shrinkage. The three samples we had fired and the remaining unfired piece all fit together well. The grog and sand effectively minimized the shrinkage in firing, but these additives to the clay could not completely prevent the warping and cracking of the figures during drying.

A last problem concerns the crackle of the black glaze surface (see Plates xiv and xix). Professor Cagiano had claimed that it was the result of a special siccative varnish,[19] and Fioravanti attributed it to the burnishing of the unfired surface with an agate tool. In reality it should be explained in the same way as the similar phenomenon on Corinthian and other vases that have a poorly adhering glaze which often peels or flakes. The crackle is caused by the difference of the coefficient of expansion of the glaze and the clay body; during firing the clay body expanded and contracted at a rate different from that of the glaze, forcing the glaze to crackle.

In summary, the technical study of the terracotta warriors established that manganese had been used as a coloring agent, a material that was not used in the classical lands of ancient times. The figures were fired in one stage only, an oxidizing atmosphere, rather than by the three-stage process of Greek and Etruscan practice. The careful provision for the ventilation of the clay by an adequate number of ventholes, common to authentic ancient terracottas, had been overlooked in the construction of the statues. Structurally, they exhibited evidence of never having stood intact as finished pieces of sculpture. Although the warriors were acquired by the Museum over forty years ago, one of the forgers corroborated all of the conclusions deduced by technical analysis.

19. See above, page 12, note 16.

SPECTROGRAPHIC ANALYSES
OF GENUINE AND FALSE
ETRUSCAN TERRACOTTAS

Analyses of Genuine Etruscan Terracottas

	Bucchero	Boccanera Slab in London	Campana Slab in the Louvre	Terracotta Statue from Veii in the Villa Giulia		Architectural Terracotta New York X. 379	
	CLAY BODY	CLAY BODY	GLAZE	GLAZE	CLAY BODY	GLAZE	CLAY BODY
Silicon	Major	Major	Major	Major	Major	Major	Major
Aluminum	Major	Major	Minor	Major	Major	Minor	Minor
Manganese	0.0X, low	0.X, low	0.X, low	0.0X	0.0X	0.X	0.X
Iron	Major, low	Major, low	Minor	Major, low	Major, low	Minor	Minor
Magnesium	0.X	Major, low	0.X	Minor	Minor	0.X	0.X
Titanium	0.X	0.X	0.X	Minor	Minor	0.X	0.X
Lead	0.00X	0.X	0.0X	0.0X	0.0X	0.00X	0.00X
Copper	0.0X	0.00X	0.00X	0.00X, low	0.00X, low	0.00X	0.00X
Nickel	0.00X	0.0X	Not found	0.00X	0.00X	Not found	Not found
Tin	Not found	Not found	"	Not found	Not found	"	"
Bismuth	"	"	"	"	"	"	"
Antimony	"	"	"	"	"	"	"
Arsenic	"	"	"	"	"	"	"
Zinc	"	"	"	"	"	"	"
Cadmium	"	"	"	"	"	"	"
Indium	"	"	"	"	"	"	"
Cobalt	"	"	"	"	"	"	"
Chromium	0.00X	"	"	"	"	"	"
Molybdenum	Not found	"	"	"	"	"	"
Vanadium	"	"	"	"	"	"	"
Tungsten	"	"	"	"	"	"	"
Silver	Not checked	"	0.0X	"	"	"	"
Potassium	Minor	0.X	Not checked	Minor	Minor	"	"
Calcium	0.X, high	Minor, high	Not found	Minor	Minor	0.X	0.X, low
Barium	0.X	0.X	Not checked	0.0X	Minor	Not found	Not found
Sodium	0.X	0.X, high	Minor	0.0X	0.0X	0.X, low	"
Strontium	0.00X	0.X	Not checked	Not found	0.X	Not found	"

NOTE: Major = above 5% estimated. Minor = 1–5% estimated. .X, .0X, .00X, etc. = concentration of the elements estimated to the nearest decimal place—*e.g.*, .0X = .01–.09% estimated. The detectability varies considerably among the elements and also depends upon the amount and nature of the sample. "Not found," therefore, means not detected in the particular sample by the technique employed.

APPENDIX B

Analyses of the Terracotta Warriors

	The Old Warrior New York 15.164		The Colossal Head New York 16.117		The Big Warrior New York 21.195		Sample of Unfired Clay
	GLAZE	CLAY BODY	GLAZE	CLAY BODY	GLAZE	CLAY BODY	CLAY BODY
Silicon	Major	Major	Major	Major	Major	Major	Major
Aluminum	Major, low	Minor	Major	Major	Major, low	Major, low	Major
Manganese	Minor	0.X	Major, low	Major, low	Major, low	Minor	Major, low
Iron	Minor	Minor	Major, low	Major	Minor	Major, low	Major, low
Magnesium	0.X, high	Minor	Minor	Minor, high	0.X, high	Minor	Minor
Titanium	0.X	Minor	Minor	Minor	0.X	Minor	Minor
Lead	0.00X	0.00X	0.0X	0.0X	0.00X	0.00X	0.0X
Copper	0.00X	0.00X	0.0X	0.0X	0.00X	0.0X, low	0.0X
Nickel	Not found	Not found	0.00X	0.00X	0.00X	0.00X	0.0X
Tin	"	"	Not found	Not found	Not found	Not found	0.00X, low
Bismuth	"	"	"	"	"	"	Not found
Antimony	"	"	"	"	"	"	"
Arsenic	"	"	"	"	"	"	"
Zinc	"	"	"	"	"	"	"
Cadmium	"	"	"	"	"	"	"
Indium	"	"	"	"	"	"	"
Cobalt	"	"	"	"	"	"	"
Chromium	"	"	"	"	"	"	"
Molybdenum	"	"	"	"	"	"	"
Vanadium	"	"	"	"	"	"	"
Tungsten	"	"	"	"	"	"	"
Silver	"	"	"	"	"	"	0.00X, low
Potassium	Not checked	Not checked	Not checked	Not checked	Not checked	Not checked	Major, low
Calcium	0.X, low	0.X	0.X	0.X, high	0.X, low	0.X, low	Minor
Barium	Not checked	Not checked	Not checked	Not checked	Not checked	Not checked	Minor
Sodium	Not found	Not found	0.X	Minor	Not found	0.X	0.X
Strontium	Not checked	Not checked	Not checked	Not checked	Not checked	Not checked	0.X

NOTE: Major = above 5% estimated. Minor = 1–5% estimated. .X, .0X, .00X, etc. = concentration of the elements estimated to the nearest decimal place—*e.g.*, .0X = .01–.09% estimated. The detectability varies considerably among the elements and also depends upon the amount and nature of the sample. "Not found," therefore, means not detected in the particular sample by the technique employed.

APPENDIX C

Other Forgeries

| | Sea Monster Slab New York 14.105.8 | | | | | Castellani Sarcophagus in London | | Scapini Reproduction of Attic Red-figured Cup | | Copenhagen Kore H.I.N. 476 (H 845) | |
	CLAY BODY	ORANGE-YELLOW	RED	BOTTOM BLUE	TOP BLUE	GLAZE	CLAY BODY	GLAZE	CLAY BODY	GLAZE	CLAY BODY
Silicon	Major	Major	Major, low	Major	Major	Major	Major, low	Major	Major	Major	Major
Aluminum	Major	Major, low	Minor	Major, low	Major, low	Major	Major, low	Major	Major	Major	Major
Manganese	0.X	0.X	Major, low	0.X	0.X	0.X, low	0.X, low	Minor	0.X	Minor	0.0X
Iron	Major, low	Minor	Major	Minor	Minor	Major, low	Major	Minor	Major	Minor	Minor
Magnesium	Minor	Minor	Minor	Minor	Minor	Major, low	Minor	Minor	Major	0.X	Minor
Titanium	Minor	0.X	0.0X	0.X	Not found	0.X	0.X	0.X	Minor	0.00X	0.00X
Lead	0.X	0.X	0.X	Minor	0.X	Minor	0.0X	Major	Minor	0.0X	0.0X
Copper	0.X, low	0.0X	0.X	0.X, low	0.0X	0.00X	0.0X	0.X	0.0X	0.0X	0.0X
Nickel	Not found	Not found	0.0X	0.X	Not found	0.0X	0.0X	Not found	Not found	Not found	Not found
Tin	0.0X	0.00X	Not found	0.X	0.00X	0.X, low	Not found	Not checked	Not checked	0.00X, low	0.00X, low
Bismuth	Not found	Not found	"	Not found	Not found	Not found	"	Not found	Not found	Not found	Not found
Antimony	"	"	"	0.0X	"	"	"	"	"	"	"
Arsenic	"	"	"	Not found	"	"	"	"	"	"	"
Zinc	"	"	Minor	"	"	"	"	"	"	0.0X	0.0X, low
Cadmium	"	"	Not found	"	"	"	"	"	"	Not found	Not found
Indium	"	"	"	"	"	"	"	"	"	"	"
Cobalt	"	0.0X	0.X	Major, low	Major, low	0.0X	"	Minor	"	"	"
Chromium	"	Not found	Not found	0.X	0.X	Not found	"	0.0X	"	"	"
Molybdenum	"	"	"	Not found	Not found	"	"	Not found	"	"	"
Vanadium	"	"	"	"	"	"	"	"	"	"	"
Tungsten	"	"	"	"	"	"	"	"	"	"	"
Silver	0.00X	0.00X	0.00X	0.00X	"	"	"	0.00X	0.0X	0.00X	0.00X, low
Potassium	0.X	0.X	0.X	0.X	0.0X	0.X	0.X	0.0X	0.X	Minor	Minor
Calcium	Minor	Minor	0.X	Minor	0.X	Minor, high	Minor, high	0.X	Minor	0.X	0.X
Barium	Minor	Minor	0.X	Minor	Not found	0.X	0.X	Not found	Not found	Not found	Not found
Sodium	0.X	0.0X	0.0X	0.X	0.0X	0.X, high	0.X, high	0.0X	0.X, low	0.0X	0.0X
Strontium	0.X	Not found	Not found	Not found	Not found	0.X	0.X	Not found	Not found	Not found	Not found

NOTE: Major = above 5% estimated. Minor = 1 – 5% estimated. .X, .0X, .00X, etc. = concentration of the elements estimated to the nearest decimal place—*e.g.*, .0X = .01–.09% estimated. The detectability varies considerably among the elements and also depends upon the amount and nature of the sample. "Not found," therefore, means not detected in the particular sample by the technique employed.

PLATE I

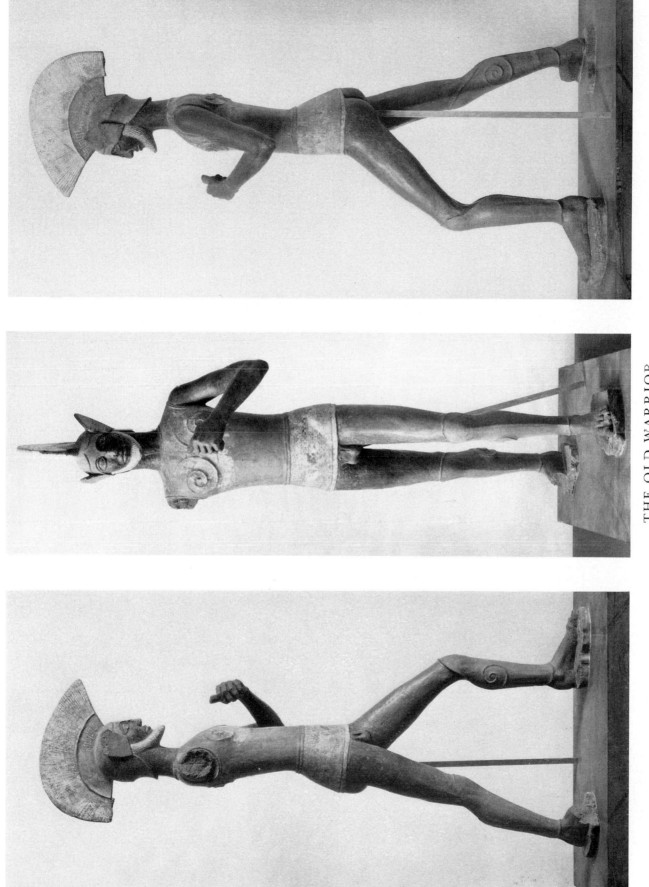

THE OLD WARRIOR
Height (without plinth) 6 feet 7¾ inches

PLATE II

A. Interior of upper half of trunk of the old warrior

C. Back view of the old warrior

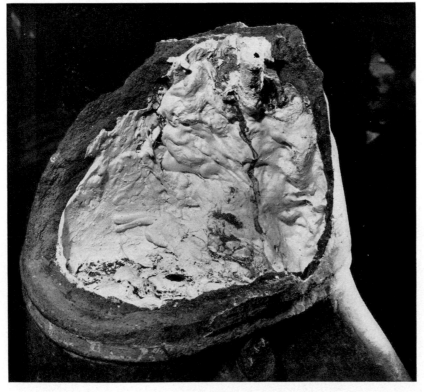

B. Interior of lower half of trunk of the old warrior

PLATE III

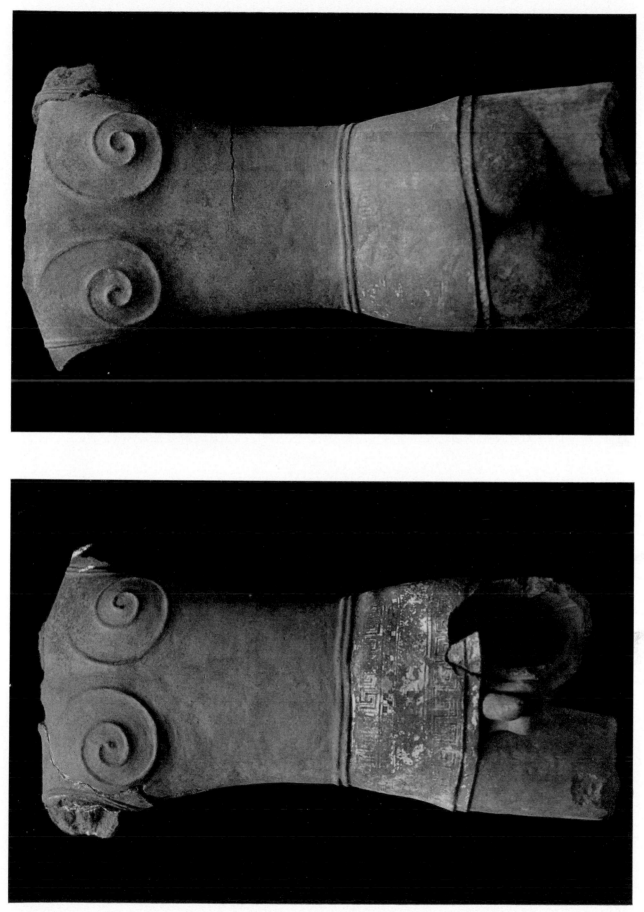

PLATE IV

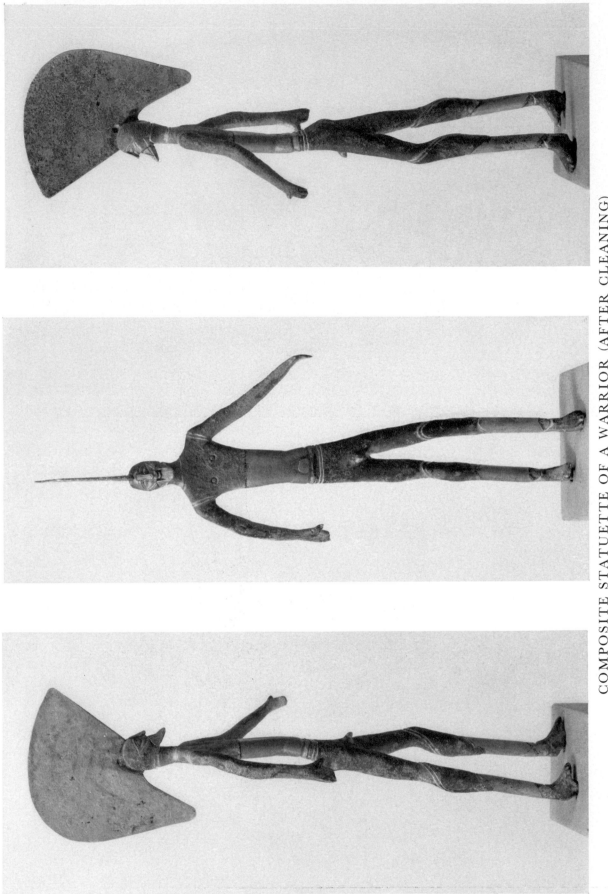

COMPOSITE STATUETTE OF A WARRIOR (AFTER CLEANING)
Bronze, with brass and copper additions. Height 10⅝ inches. New York, Metropolitan Museum, acc. no. 19.192.2

PLATE V

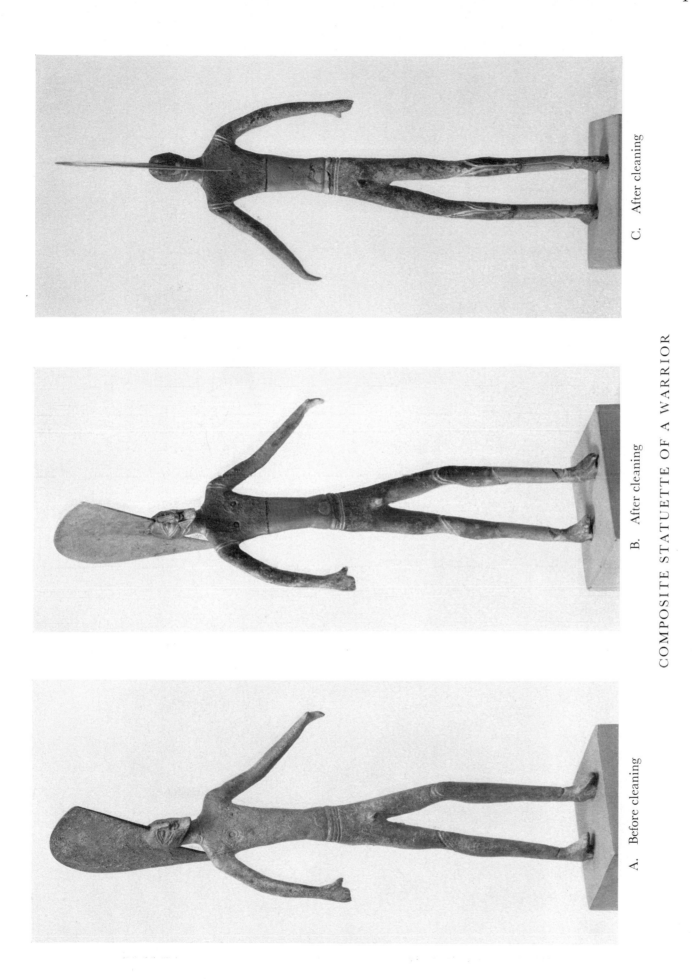

A. Before cleaning　　B. After cleaning　　C. After cleaning

COMPOSITE STATUETTE OF A WARRIOR

PLATE VI

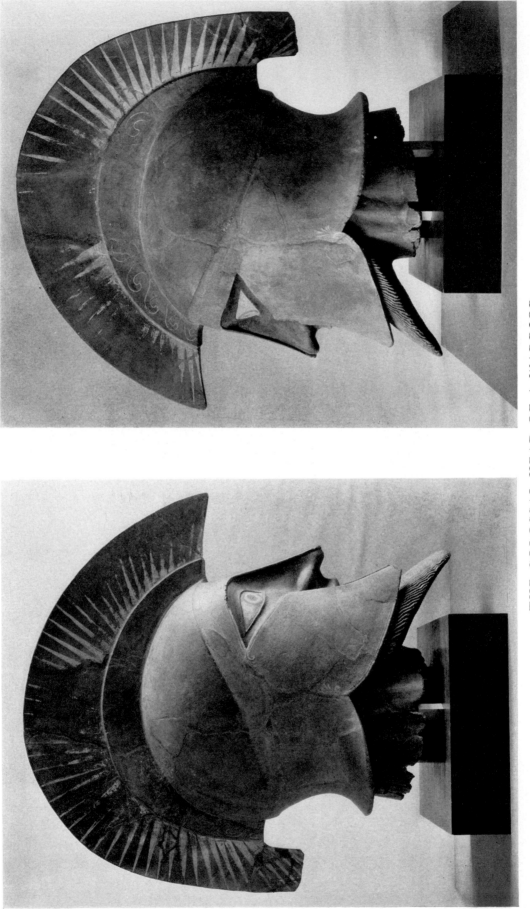

THE COLOSSAL HEAD OF A WARRIOR
Height 4 feet 7 inches

PLATE VII

B. Terracotta aryballos in the form of a helmeted head. East Greek, vi century B.C. Height 2⁹⁄₁₆ inches. New York, Metropolitan Museum, acc. ro. 21.88.170. Rogers Fund, 1921

C. Terracotta aryballos in the form of a helmeted head. East Greek, vi century B.C. Height 2⅝ inches. New York, Metropolitan Museum, acc. no. 21.88.171. Rogers Fund, 1921

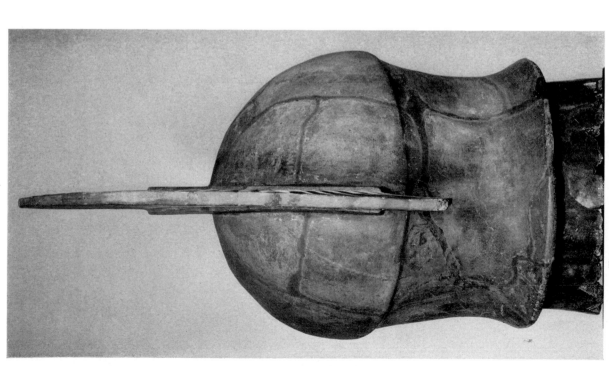

A. Back view of the colossal head

PLATE VIII

THE COLOSSAL HEAD BEFORE ARRIVAL IN NEW YORK

PLATE IX

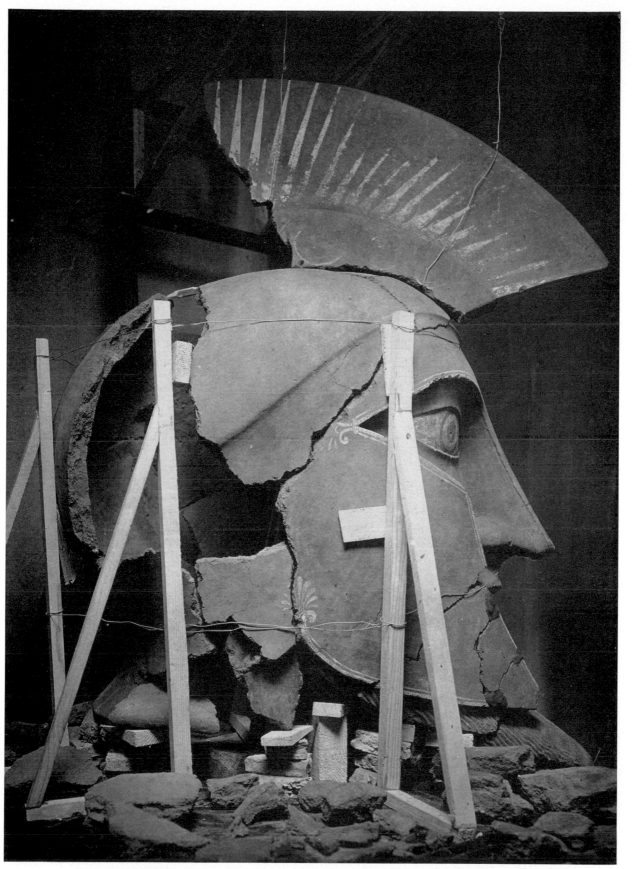

THE COLOSSAL HEAD BEFORE ARRIVAL IN NEW YORK

PLATE X

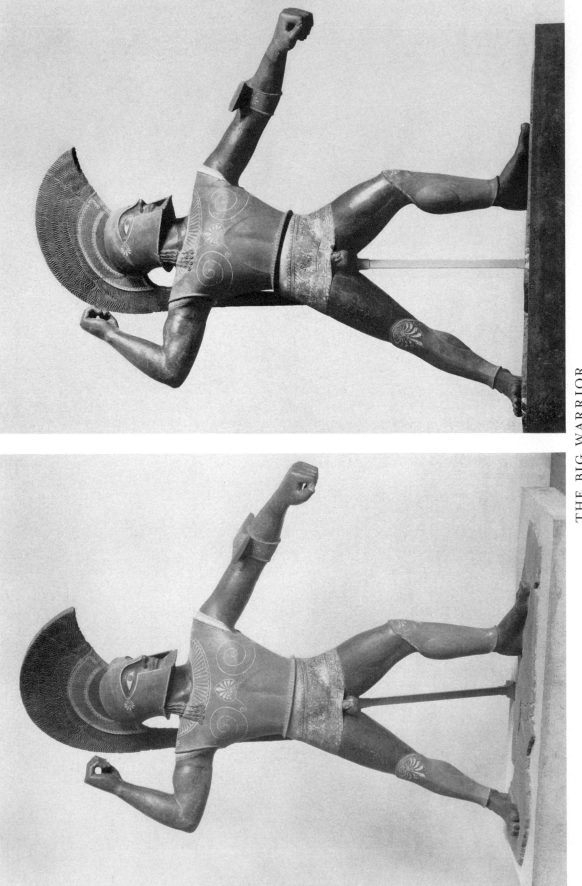

THE BIG WARRIOR
Height (without plinth) 8 feet ¼ inch

PLATE XI

THE BIG WARRIOR RECONSTRUCTED WITH
WOODEN SWORD AND SHIELD

THE BIG WARRIOR

PLATE XII

THE BIG WARRIOR BEFORE RECONSTRUCTION

PLATE XIII

THE BIG WARRIOR BEFORE RECONSTRUCTION

PLATE XIV

HEAD OF THE BIG WARRIOR

PLATE XV

B.   Head seen from below

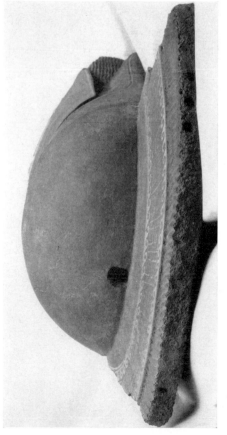

D.   Inside of torso showing drying crack across crotch

A.   Neck and shoulders

C.   Venthole on top of helmet

DETAILS OF THE BIG WARRIOR

PLATE XVI

P. BOLLO.

DRAWING BY PAUL R. BOLLO OF THE RIGHT PANEL OF THE MONTELEONE CHARIOT
(ETRUSCAN, VI CENTURY B.C.) IN THE METROPOLITAN MUSEUM

PLATE XVII

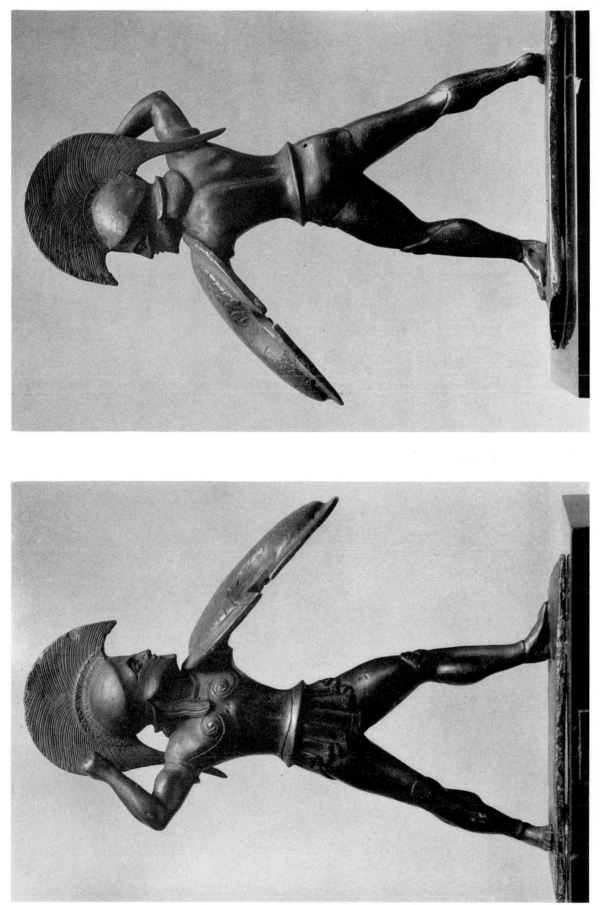

BRONZE STATUETTE OF A WARRIOR FROM DODONA
Greek, about 470 B.C. Height (without plinth) 5 inches. Berlin inv. 7470

PLATE XVIII

FRONT AND BACK VIEWS (ACTUAL SIZE) OF THE TWO TEST PIECES

PLATE XIX

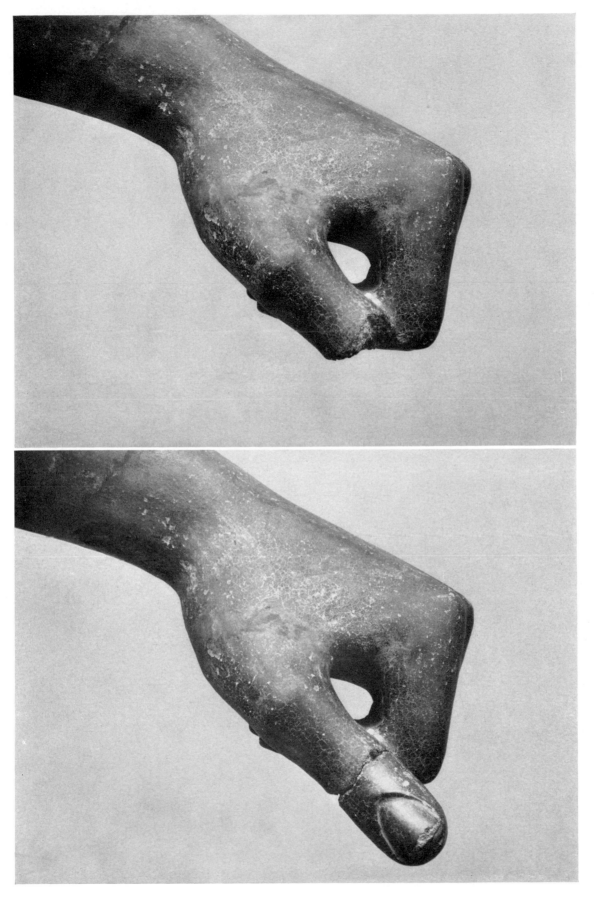

LEFT HAND OF THE BIG WARRIOR WITH AND WITHOUT THUMB

PLATE XX

Coolidge

A (left). Fragmentary terracotta statue of a woman. Height 29½ inches. New York, Metropolitan Museum, acc. no. 16.141

B (above). Terracotta bust of a woman. Height 16½ inches. Mrs. H. D. Wilmarth Collection

PLATE XXI

A (left). Terracotta bust of a woman. Etruscan (Cerveteri), iv century B.C. Height 6⅝ inches. New York, Metropolitan Museum, acc. no. 96.18.174. Purchased by subscription, 1896

B (below). Detail of an Etruscan alabaster sarcophagus in Palermo, from a drawing in G. Micali *Storia degli antichi popoli italiani*

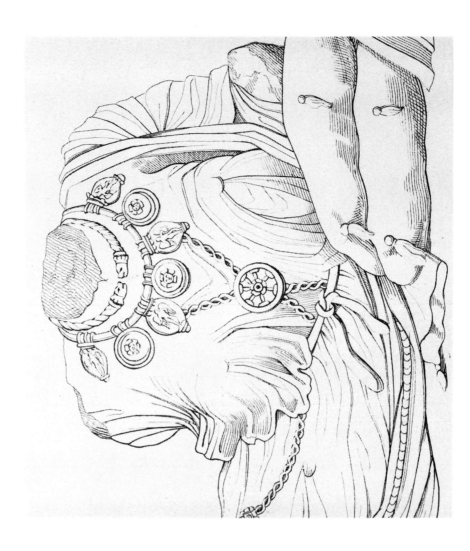

PLATE XXII

A (left). New York, Metropolitan Museum, acc. no. 14.105.8 g. Height 7 inches

B (right). Vatican inv. 13844. Etruscan, IV century B.C. Height 5 ½ inches

Andrén

C, D. Orvieto, Museo dell' Opera del Duomo. Etruscan, IV century B.C. Height 6 ⅞ inches

E. Copenhagen, Ny Carlsberg Glyptotek, I.N. 2464 (after cleaning). Etruscan, IV century B.C. Height 7 ⅞ inches

TERRACOTTA ARCHITECTURAL RELIEFS

PLATE XXIII

A (left). Brussels A 3536. Height 15¼ inches

B (right). Vatican inv. 14110. Height 18 inches

C (left). Copenhagen, National Museum, inv. 6544. Height 17¼ inches

D (right). Rome, Palazzo dei Conservatori, 7200. Height 16½ inches

Anderson

E (left). Formerly Rome, A. Signorelli Collection. Height 15 inches

F (right). Rome, Villa Giulia, 27158. Height 15 inches

TERRACOTTA ARCHITECTURAL RELIEFS

PLATE XXIV

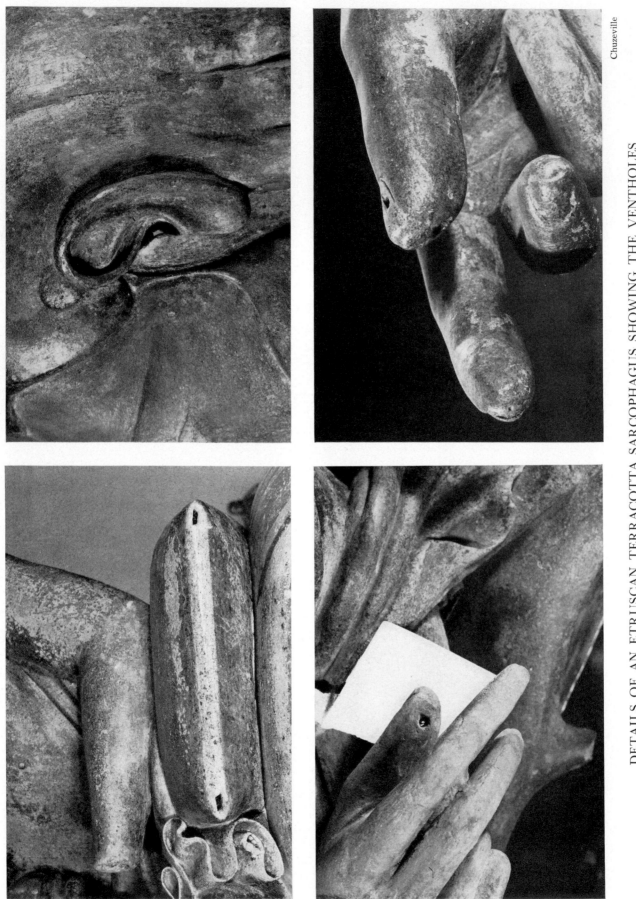

Chuzeville

DETAILS OF AN ETRUSCAN TERRACOTTA SARCOPHAGUS SHOWING THE VENTHOLES

Paris, Louvre, inv. Campana 5194